THE BEAUTY AND NOBILITY OF LIFE

THE BEAUTY AND NOBILITY OF LIFE

THE RESTORATION OF MEANING IN A WORLD OVERWHELMED BY COMMERCIALISM, SCIENTISM, AND FUNDAMENTALISM

ANDREW CORT, JD, DC

Introduction by Stephen Larsen, PhD

Includes Bibliographical References and Index

ISBN-13: 978-1533314079
ISBN-10: 1533314071

PRINTED IN THE UNITED STATES OF AMERICA

Cover photograph of Taylor Lake on the Colgate University campus by
P. Guttenberg

For Megan

ALSO BY ANDREW CORT

Symbols, Meaning, and the Sacred Quest
*Spiritual Awakening in Jewish, Christian
and Islamic Stories*

Love, Wisdom, and God
The Longing of the Western Soul

The Sacred Chalice – Women of the Bible
*The Psychological and Spiritual Meaning
of Their Stories*

The Door is Open
*The 7 Steps of Spiritual Awakening that Western
Scripture and Mythology Have Been Trying
to Tell Us All Along*

Eat Healthy
Live Longer, Live Kinder

From Joshua to Jesus
*A Brief Chronicle of the Kings, Empires, Legends
and Ideas, that Paved the Way to Bethlehem*

Our Healing Birthright
Taking Responsibility for Ourselves and Our Planet

Our duty, as men and women, is to proceed
as if limits to our ability did not exist.
We are collaborators in creation.

- Teilhard de Chardin

TABLE OF CONTENTS

INTRODUCTION

by Stephen Larsen, PhD

Tis sweet little book could and should be read by everyone. Andrew Cort in his previous eight offerings has honed an elegantly simple style that is accessible to a high-school senior: but for the thoughtful and highly literate reader, the profundity of his thoughts and the reach of his intellect seize your interest, and intrigue you to follow his flow of thinking.

As the book moves from "what went wrong" to what can "come 'round right," we are led on a spiral dance that follows the sacred geometry laid out in the Renaissance *Book of the Twenty Four Philosophers:* "God is an intelligible sphere whose center is everywhere, and circumference is nowhere!" That is to say, Dr. Cort takes us on a clearly spiritual journey without excessive mention of the belabored term "God," or any preachy rhetoric.

He starts out from a painful place that I have spent a number of years trying to limn for myself and for the literate public, eventuating in my 2007 book *The Fundamentalist Mind.* The book arose from my agony of the soul about how something as seemingly beautiful as religion can become one of the major divisive forces that incites violence, and tears the world apart. Dr. Cort mentions the theologian Reinhold Niebuhr, who knew that we need to take religion seriously, but not literally. My long-term mentor and friend, Joseph Campbell, put it this way: "Half the people in the world think that the metaphors of their religious traditions...are facts...and we have others who classify themselves as atheists because they think religious metaphors are lies.... Which group really gets the message?" (from *Thou Art That,* also quoted by Cort.)

Andrew Cort is no stranger to rigorous thinking; he went from being a teacher of mathematics and physics, to a licensed healer (doctor of chiropractic), to a practicing attorney, and then, in later years. returning to chiropractic and being ordained as an interfaith minister, in which his main plea is for religious tolerance in our contentious world – but without a simplistic wooly-minded inclusiveness, thank you very much. We must learn to think, he exhorts us throughout the book, with the precision of Plato, like Kant and Schopenhauer, like the architects of the American Constitution, like Emerson, while still affirming "the beauty and nobility of life."

To establish "where we went wrong," Cort goes back to the *urgrund*, the underlying paradigm of Western culture, and its outcomes. It may have been in literalizing Democritus' atoms and hurrying particles of matter everywhere, or Descartes, who insisted we are apart from nature as mere "beholders," or Newton, who articulated very useful laws of mechanics that we use every day, but that don't apply to dimensions beyond the human scale – the vast cosmology of astrophysics or the infinitesimal particles of quantum mechanics. Humanity changes the *content* of its thought, going from religion to post-Enlightenment science, but not the *style* of its thinking, in that modern *scientism* is just as dogmatic and "fundamentalist" as the religion that preceded it. Neither "popular science," nor the view of the universe based on it, has gone much beyond 10th grade science, in which force and coercion are the dynamics, rather than subtlety, indeterminacy, "fields of effect," and relativity, which are far better descriptions of "the way things really work". (Nothing can pretend to be an ultimate description either of the way the universe works, or who or what God is for that matter, but why shouldn't our closest approximations be based on our best and latest science?)

Dr. Cort shows us how our view of the universe affects everything we do, from the way we treat nature, to animals, to each other, to ourselves. A misreading of *Genesis* says we white Europeans must assert *domination* over nature, and even over "more primitive" peoples such as Africans or Native Americans, rather than accepting the peaceful

12

responsibility of having *dominion*. (Conservative political commentator Ann Coulter outspokenly asserts that the Bible gave us permission to "dominate" the North American continent, all its resources, species, and indigenous inhabitants – which leads us as if caught in a terrible world-annihilating spell, step by step to the ecological disaster we now find ourselves in, as well as the genocides we have committed.) These paradigms are so fundamental that they easily lend themselves to a blithe and unconscious materialistic fundamentalism, out of which come excesses and harmful depredations on the ecosystem, our fellow creatures, and other people.

My own inescapable example of this is connected to my livelihood as a health professional, and it is a topic Cort also goes into, just as he does the educational and social fundamentalisms: that is to say, the application of the mechanistic paradigm to the human body and its nervous system. For my part, I deal with patients affected by traumatic brain injury (TBI) or post-traumatic-stress-disorder (PTSD), and a raft of other problems covered in the DSM-V: anxiety, depression, addictions. Although these people are clearly affected in their bodies and souls (the Greek word psyche means "soul") they feel the medical paradigm treats them as "machines" or "bags of chemicals" to which prescription drugs should be added to rectify chemical imbalances. They are not related to as "thou" nor invited to participate as intelligent, living dynamical systems in their own "cure."

Although this book does not shirk from the many problems that currently beset our species, there is nonetheless a palpable optimism throughout; as if somehow Andrew Cort believes that humanity can realize its own essential goodness – can come to that innate ethical knowing Plato calls the *Nous* – a faculty of innate and direct knowing of what is truly good and beautiful present in every human being. I am reminded of my friend Michael Schacker's *Global Awakening*, in which, in spite of detailing everything wrong in our greedy, gullible, suicidal culture, he affirms that a new "organic shift" is not only possible, but an actual certainty, because our world has always been transformed by such collective *metanoias* – from the Sixth Century BCE, with Lao Tzu, the Buddha, and Zoroaster, through the time of Christ, the Renaissance, the Enlightenment, and that amazing period of our last century called "the sixties" when a whole new re-appreciation of the environment, original peoples such as the Native Americans, and vast panoramas of the mind opened by the consciousness revolution appeared.

I finish this brief introduction to Andrew Cort's important new work with a poem by Rilke that seems to describe his developmental journey:

The Ancient Tower

I live my life in growing orbits,
that move out over the things of this world.
I do not know if I shall achieve the last,
but that will be my intent!
I am circling around God, around the Ancient Tower,
and still I do not know,
If I am a falcon, or a storm, or a great song!

***

Stephen Larsen, PhD, LMHC, is Professor Emeritus of Psychology at SUNY Ulster, board-certified in EEG biofeedback, and is the author of several books, including *A Fire in the Mind: The Life of Joseph Campbell* (the authorized biography, written together with his wife Robin), *The Fundamentalist Mind, The Mythic Imagination,* and *The Neurofeedback Solution.* Dr. Larsen is the founder and director of The Center for Symbolic Studies, as well as Stone Mountain Center (offering biofeedback, neurofeedback, and psychotherapy treatments). The Larsens live in New Paltz, NY.

CHAPTER ONE

WHAT WENT WRONG?

In this extraordinary time, when so many of us are blessed with unlimited freedom, an endless variety of technological wonders, an ever-increasing life expectancy, easy access to knowledge and education, and an abundance of leisure and entertainment, many of us endure a disquieting sense of meaninglessness and emptiness. We are free, but free to do what? We own all sorts of amazing things, they make our lives easy and they keep us entertained, but to what end? We can talk to anyone anywhere at any moment, but what is there to say? What is the point of it all?

If there is a genuine meaning inherent in life – not just a personally-posited goal but an objectively true significance to it all – this implies there is something that transcends our daily concerns. In earlier times, a world rich with this sort of meaning was part of everyone's normal experience. The sharp difference that we ascribe to secular matters and sacred matters could never make sense to a Shaman. The gods and goddesses of Homer's Greece were part of everyone's daily life. In the Garden of Eden, God walked about and talked to the inhabitants. He spoke with Abraham and Moses, and later sent His son into the world.

In these times and cultures, people believed they were immersed in a sacred world, they knew who and what they were, and most importantly they felt a direct participation in higher levels of existence that gave their lives purpose and value. But for the most part, writes Douglas Sloan, during the last three or four centuries "this participatory awareness of a meaningful world has dimmed almost to the point of extinction."[1]

At the same time, something very positive has emerged in its place: the modern development and strengthening of individual selfhood. We experience the self's relationship to the world in a very different way than our ancestors. We have a far greater sense of personal identity, separate from others and detached from nature. We demand and expect personal freedom and full opportunity for personal achievement.

But modern individuals are no longer sustained by a living and sacred world. We find ourselves grounded instead in the 'onlooker' viewpoint of science in which we analyze nature from the outside and find ways to make her do our bidding. We have been phenomenally successful at this, and our intelligence and creativity continue to bear fruit every day. It is also true, however, that we endure the psychological consequences of holding to this position: alienation, fragmentation, loss of meaning. Nothing characterizes the modern world more completely than the loss of an intuitive understanding of transcendence, our lack of appreciation for levels of reality above our everyday affairs. By shutting the door on transcendence, we have cut off any light from that world that might have illuminated this one, leaving us in darkness, leaving us with nothing but a dead world where scientists are merely performing an autopsy.

Must this be the inevitable outcome of the modern experiment in individualization? Is the apex of this endeavor merely the bleak realization that the individual is alone in a meaningless, violent and absurd universe? Or is it possible to remain a free and rational 'self', and still be connected to a living web of mutuality and authentic meaning?

Fundamentalism

One way that people attempt to hold on to meaning and avoid the despair of emptiness, is to simply reject the prevalent scientific worldview and revert to religious fundamentalism, which insists that all the profound teachings of one's religious tradition must be believed literally and in every instance, that no other source of knowledge is valid, and everyone must be brought into total compliance. This, of course, is completely contrary to the ideals of personal freedom and individual selfhood. Yet fundamentalism is becoming more and more widespread in today's world, from Islamic fundamentalists in the Middle East to Born-Again Christians in America. Interestingly, Sloan points out that fundamentalism's "turning of past teachings of great complexity and delicate nuance concerning the spirit into literal statements about the world", is ironically dependent upon the acceptance of a major tenet of the dreaded contemporary positivistic science. That is, fundamentalists actually have to *agree* with these scientists that the only true knowledge which is possible or worthwhile consists of literal statements of fact about the empirical world.

> Thus does literalism kill the spirit. In a misconstrued effort to maintain a connection with that mysterious source of meaning and significance, mystery is destroyed and made banal and pedestrian. [2]

So rather than restoring a sense of meaning to the world, fundamentalism, of whatever stripe, accomplishes the opposite. Even worse, when fear of the loss of one's tradition fuses with anger at those deemed to be threatening it, fundamentalism justifies all manner of ugliness and oppression. Here is born so much of the violence in today's world, all in the name of irrational beliefs, "traditional teachings hardened and drained of their wisdom."[3] In this way, fundamentalism angers and disgusts many thoughtful and compassionate people, and turns their hearts and minds away from anything reeking of spirituality since the agenda of 'fundamentalism' is often mistakenly considered to be synonymous with 'religion'. But they are not the same thing. Religious fundamentalism, writes Stephen Larsen, "takes the luminous and mythic, whose realm is meant to be metaphor and symbol, and imprisons it in matter and history."[4] (Perhaps even more importantly, Larsen reminds us that fundamentalist thinking, which typically means *not* thinking for oneself but unquestioningly believing what one has been told, is not limited to spiritual matters. It also makes its way into our beliefs about science, economics, politics, art, and all manner of things we care about. "All fundamentalisms are not religious or mythic," he notes. "Many are secular and materialistic. It is not the *content* in these cases, so much as the absolutist *style* of conviction and expression that betrays their fundamentalist nature."[5] This absolutist way of thinking – and that is what it is: *a way of thinking* – is at the root of much divisiveness and contempt in today's world.)

~

A more moderate attempt to maintain a sense of meaning, that is employed by many sophisticated modern people, is to grant that empirical scientific knowledge is acceptable and good, and so is a concern with the realm of meaning and value. But they are kept in two separate and unrelated mental compartments, and the latter is regarded benignly as little more than a collection of irrational feelings and naïve aspirations. This approach allows the two realms to coexist, but it mostly just distracts us from confronting the painful issue while giving *no real weight* to the idea that there is meaning and purpose in existence – it simply "appreciates" things like art and poetry and religion, in a pleasant self-satisfying sort of way, usually during a Sunday afternoon visit to the museum. It encourages a modicum of respect for human values, but because it refuses to accord them equal status with "solid scientific knowledge", the whole project is difficult, if not pointless, to sustain.

~

At the opposite end of the spectrum is the 'New Age' movement. Unlike fundamentalism, which limits all possible knowledge to *one* teaching, the movement typically insists on including *every tradition possible.* But in doing so, it ends up watering them down and exploiting them. It conveniently takes from other cultures whatever ideas and practices seem interesting and stimulating, with little regard for the complete, integrated framework of these traditions. This borrowing of attractive bits and pieces from other cultures, torn from their context of history and meaning, is degrading to the traditions themselves (since it does not really take them seriously) as well as ultimately useless to the borrower. The Buddhist scholar Lama Govinda, for instance, describes how Zen then tends to become nothing but "an excuse to live as one always did, only giving different labels to the same actions: waywardness will be made into spontaneity, weakness into the principle of non-violence, laziness into the ideal of non-action, lack of logic into spiritual profundity."[6]

Here, then, we still find no useful solution to our modern dilemma. None of these things solve the problem of meaninglessness – and the problem runs even deeper.

Commercialism

In the years immediately following World War II, a remarkable shift occurred in American economic life. For the first time in history, we reached a stage of prosperous development in which we could produce far more goods and services than anyone needed. Various factors combined to create this new situation, including advanced industrial technology, wartime expansion of the economy, the destruction of Europe's industrial base while our own remained unscathed, and women added to the workforce. To sustain all this growth, to continue paying wages and expanding profits, it became necessary to stimulate our habits of consumption, to artificially increase the public's appetite for what was being produced. No longer could manufacturers rest content with simply determining what people wanted and needed. Thenceforward, to a degree never witnessed before, it became necessary to learn effective ways of persuading people that they wanted and needed all sorts of things that they had never wanted or needed before. As a result, the public was soon being bombarded with non-stop messages to fall in line and do what we were being told: the duty of Americans, it became clear, was to go shopping. The pursuit of the 'good life' had been confused with accumulating the 'goods'.

Just as advertisers were beginning to seek out scientific advice to help them develop more effective methods and procedures for what was casually called 'engineering consent', television appeared on the scene. Soon the nation was practically catatonic. Consumers became targets rather than individuals, and the professional persuaders began using heavy artillery. Rather than explaining a product's quality or usefulness, they concentrated on ways to manipulate our suggestibility, our fears, our least becoming motivations. Using every technique they could garner from science, advertisers soon computerized vast amounts of information about our personal lives and buying habits as discerned from focus groups, psychological interviewing techniques, brain-wave measurements, studies of reactions to various sounds and pictures, etc.

But it continued to become increasingly difficult to reach people in the midst of the exploding carnival of marketing and promotion, so as consumers became more jaded the marketers became even more aggressive. To accommodate the ever-increasing number of things to be sold, advertisements had to become ever briefer. The effect of this was to shorten the public's already meager attention span: an image has to hit home deeply and instantly or it will never be noticed. More importantly, it soon became apparent that this is best accomplished by evoking negative emotions such as anxiety, fear and envy which is a far cry from simply distributing useful information about products, which require a buyer's time and thoughtfulness. The goal was clear: consumers needed to think less and buy more.

A further consequence of this new consumer culture was that it became necessary for us to become a nation of waste-makers. With so much being produced, we have to continually discard the old to make room for the new. The promise of instant gratification is necessary, but the

20

economy will stall if products gratify for too long. It is therefore necessary for things to become obsolete or break down quickly and need to be thrown away and replaced.

With the general public virtually hypnotized into supporting these trends, more and more wealth was accumulating into fewer and fewer hands, giving big American business immense power to determine conditions here and around the world. This awesome financial power linked up with exuberant postwar feelings of patriotism and manifest destiny, and soon the American public was convinced that anything that interfered with the expansion of American corporate power was un-American (we are still bearing the ugly consequences of this pseudo-patriotism today, perhaps more so than ever). Thus began the incessant and peculiar identification of Freedom with Capitalism.[*]

To maintain overwhelming public support for corporate America, public relations experts were brought in. The public needed to receive the appropriate messages, not just from advertising, but from the arts, entertainment, government, schools, museums, libraries, churches, and eventually the internet – in short, from all avenues of modern culture. Now, in consequence, our lives are immersed in a steady stream of repetitive, continuous propaganda, perpetuating various myths of economics, politics and science, and steadily eroding our individuality and our ability to think for ourselves.

Victor Frankl, who believed that the search for *meaning*, not the gratification of drives and instincts, is the primary motivating force in human life, once noted that for people in our modern world, "No instinct tells him what he has to do, and no tradition tells him what he ought to do; sometimes he does not even know what he wishes to do. Instead, he either wishes to do what other people do (conformism) or he does what other people wish him to do (totalitarianism)."[7] This state of mind is fertile ground for propaganda – which is not

---

[*] For America's Founders, the principle of freedom primarily meant *freedom of thought* – the freedom to pursue knowledge, truth and wisdom for oneself, without any religious or political constraints.

concerned with what is best in men and women, it is not concerned with noble feelings or admirable goals. "Propaganda", wrote Jacques Ellul, "does not aim to elevate man, but to make him *serve.*"

> It must therefore utilize the most common feelings, the most widespread ideas, the crudest patterns, and in so doing place itself on a very low level with regard to what it wants men to do and to what end. Hate, hunger, and pride make better levers of propaganda than do love or impartiality.[8]

The hatred can be leveled against immigrants, Muslims, blacks, women, Jews – it does not really matter, so long as the propagandist can arouse anger and negativity amongst the gullible and the fearful, who will then be ready to carry out instructions and toe the line.

For these and many other reasons, we now live in a culture in which style has achieved primacy over substance. Although the original conception of democracy meant that social equality was more important than a social elite, and therefore the symbols of an elite were rejected, we have now substituted the contorted alternative view that the symbols and styles of elites should be mass produced and made available to everyone. When Thomas Jefferson spoke of the "pursuit of happiness" he was referring to a spiritual, moral, and intellectual pursuit, but this has now been degraded into nothing more than a demand to satisfy any and every physical appetite, while the American ideal of equality has come to mean that we all have an equal right to possess the same stuff. Of course, the resulting mass production implies mass standardization, and thus any genuine uniqueness which was available when production meant handicraft has now been replaced by the 'sameness' of what is available to everyone. It is normal for middle school children to all want to be the 'same', to have all the same things their friends have. But this is not an appropriate way of life for adults, certainly not in a democracy that claims to value individuals.

We see the powerful mesmerizing effects of advertising and public relations in the pursuit of the perfect car, the perfe ct body, the perfect house, the perfect mate. We see it in our participation in certain activities, and our passive adherence to certain beliefs, that make us acceptable to whatever crowd we wish to join. We continue to speak proudly and sentimentally of our great respect for 'rugged individualism', but large-scale contemporary production, trade, and consumption require centralized authority, massive planning, and a willingness of so-called individuals to become cogs in the economic machine. A community of genuine individuals, held together by love, is thus transformed into an efficient ant hill, held together by money and power.

In addition to any legitimate help we may be offering to politically oppressed people in their struggles against totalitarian regimes, we insist that they emulate our strange way of life. As part of the bargain for receiving our military aid, we rip apart the tapestry of their traditions and culture, sweep away their customs and individuality, and then offer them 'modern technology and free trade of consumer goods' in return, thus ensuring that their lives can soon become as empty and alienated as our own: "For a zoned-out, stupefied populace," notes Morris Berman, "democracy will be nothing more than the right to shop, or to choose between Wendy's and Burger King, or to stare at CNN and think that this managed infotainment is actually the news."[9]

But contrary to the complaints of many critics of capitalism, the chief responsibility for all of this does not lie with Madison Avenue or the lords of corporate power. The responsibility lies squarely with *us*, with our own 'suggestibility' – that most unbecoming and ultimately most destructive of all negative human qualities: the astonishing ease with which we abdicate all efforts to think and reason for ourselves, and believe whatever we are told.

~

Life in ancient and medieval times was not enviable. There may have been a deeper sense of meaning in the world, but it is also true that life was awash with poverty, disease, early death, endless work, crime, cruelty, and war. The ancients had talked about virtue and happiness, but they never found a way to achieve these things for more than a few aristocrats. The political concern of the Enlightenment was to finally alter this. Rather than a world of countless suffering serfs, and a few princes living in luxury off of everyone else's labor, a magnificent humanitarian endeavor was undertaken to lift suffering humanity and provide a good life for all.

To bring about this enormous change there would be a cost. To attain security and prosperity for everyone we would have to stop talking about unattainable *virtue* and focus instead on accepting, understanding, and caring about human beings *as they are*. In other words, it was necessary to have an underlying philosophical change as well as a change in material conditions. Instead of thinking about ways to *transcend* the mundane realities of life, philosophers would have to become the *allies* of the day-to-day world. The human Mind would have to come down from its lofty perch and stop seeking after virtue, truth and beauty, so that the Body of humanity could be lifted up to a more suitable and just material state. The value of this endeavor is undeniable, and we rightly continue to this day to make efforts that will hopefully bring about its fulfillment for all human beings. This is the actual and appropriate task of modern commercial society, struggling toward freedom, equality, and prosperity.

But the cost has been enormous. While our human appetites and cravings still persist, the virtues that ruled them have been abandoned, leaving the body and its needs to do as they wish. It often seems that the only remaining virtue is *self-interest*. Everything else has been debunked. Our actions can only be judged according to their *utility*: do they

24

help preserve and bring comfort to the individual? "Life, Liberty, and Property" were not the concern of ancient philosophers. Their concern was with the perfection of the soul. But as philosophers and political scientists became exclusively concerned with alleviating worldly human suffering, the soul quietly disappeared.

Life was better, but somehow empty. People needed more. So a new concept was invented in response to the banality of a purely commercial life. It is called *Culture* – a vague concept that refers to aspects of life that are somehow 'higher', more intellectual, or *at least different*, than the merely physical and economic aspects. But 'culture' is not a commensurate replacement for what was lost. In the hierarchy of importance, commerce replaced patriotism, science replaced religion. People are willing to strive and fight and even die for God, for country, or any of several other virtues. In a myriad of ways, we are certainly better off as these fanaticisms die down. But the new hierarchy leaves little in life to be passionate about. Surely there is still something good to be said for human striving and heroism. But no one is willing to die for culture.

Thus, the Enlightenment agenda of open-minded scientific inquiry and the unfettered exercise of human reason has been overwhelmed by commercialism and turned into scientism and group-think. The original American dream was to strip away all the dead weight and oppressiveness of religion and politics, and create a social way of life based on reason and high principles where men and women could live in peace and pursue what Plato called "the Good". Now this has all been replaced with a debased reinterpretation about owning many unnecessary things and satisfying our never-ending physical desires. Worse yet, those who are most successful in this banal pursuit are 'free' to trample on the rest. We even regard them as 'celebrities' and look up to them

In ancient Greece, from pure speculation, Democritus and Leucippus devised a scientific theory nearly identical in many important respects to modern Atomic Theory, and simultaneously gave birth to the philosophies of Materialism and Determinism.

They began by stating that an infinite number of particles, which they called 'atoms', were the basic constituents of everything (the implication being that these tiny particles are *real* and *important,* as opposed to the world we see and experience which is merely *appearance,* and is therefore less real and less important) and these atoms were all made of the same *uniformly identical* solid material substance. They varied from each other only in size and shape.

Earlier attempts to theorize the basic components of matter had imagined different categories of particles that had different *qualities*. Particles of fire, for example, would be qualitatively different from particles of water. Different qualities cause us to have different subjective responses: fire may feel warm and pleasant and we 'like' it, or it may feel hot and painful and we 'dislike' it.

But the atoms of Democritus had no such differentiating qualities. The only differences between atoms had to do with *quantity*, not quality. Quantities are *objective* characteristics which can be measured, weighed, or counted – weight, speed, or shape, for example. These objective characteristics are not matters of opinion. *Qualities* like 'warmth' can be debated: a person coming in from a snowstorm into a sixty degree room might say "it feels warm", while a person coming out of a sauna into the very same room might disagree and say "it feels cold". But there is no debate when it comes to a *quantity*: sixty degrees is sixty degrees, whether measured by this person or that one, irrespective of how it makes us 'feel'. The only characteristics attributable to Democritus' atoms were just such *quantitative*, measurable, objective characteristics.

Even thoughts, according to Democritus, and even the human soul, were made of atoms moving about in a void. Atoms and the void were all that really existed: everything else was merely subjective *appearance*. "A thing merely appears to have color, it merely appears to be sweet or bitter," he said. "Only atoms and the void have real existence."[10]

No explanation but mechanical 'necessity' was offered to account for the motion of the atoms: they simply move about, colliding with each other and bouncing apart, always conforming to measurable laws of motion. The universe is thus a kind of colossal pinball machine. And here is the point: Things do not happen because of Zeus, or Fate, or because of any sort of intelligence, purpose, or design. Nature is not alive, it is not intertwined with divinity. Things exist, things change, things happen, solely because of blind, unalterable, mechanical necessity. This is a pure Determinism. *Even our feelings, thoughts, and beliefs*, are explained away by the Atomists in purely material terms.

As a key to understanding nature, Atomism was brilliant. Magnificent in its simplicity, breathtaking in its sweep, it explained both permanency (what things *are*) and change (what things *do*). In its refined modern revival, it has led to all the practical potency of modern science. At the same time, however, it has had far-reaching implications that are not always satisfactory to human reason. If our thoughts and feelings consist of nothing but atoms moving about in the void, then like everything else these things are merely the predetermined consequences of automatic and inflexible rules of simple mechanical necessity. The possibility of 'free will' is thus destroyed, and with it goes the entire notion of ethics: it is absurd and futile to tell someone how they should behave if they are not free to do it. Along with individual free will, Atomism deprives the human race in general of any particular significance: our presence here on earth is simply a matter of chance, an interesting but unnecessary fluke.

Additional serious consequences of the atomic theory arise from its requirement that all of reality must be reduced to the realm of *quantity*. Science owes much of its success to the reductive analytical method, which assumes that small phenomena are the 'real' constituents of the universe, and that they explain all the large 'apparent' phenomena. This method has been extremely effective, allowing us to intervene and predict nature's processes with great clarity and power. But difficulties arise when Nature is broken apart into small, quantifiable, constituents, and living things are 'explained away' in terms of non-living components. *Wholeness disappears*. Only the parts remain. And as Douglas Sloan explains, "With the disappearance of wholeness, meaning also vanishes. The connective tissue of experience, the network of intricate qualitative relationships that constitute the whole of life and make meaning and significance possible, disintegrates."[11]

Albert Einstein reflected on all this separateness and meaninglessness in a letter to a friend:

> A human being is a part of the whole, called by us 'Universe,' a part limited in time and space. He experiences himself, his thoughts and feelings as something separate from the rest – a kind of optical delusion of his consciousness. The striving to free oneself from this delusion is the one issue of true religion. Not to nourish it but to try to overcome it is the way to reach the attainable measure of peace of mind.[12]

In addition to losing sight of the whole, the Atomic outlook also loses sight of *qualities*, considering them to be essentially unreal and inconsequential. Like 'wholeness', however, the realm of *quality* is a source of human meaning. But in the world presented by the Atomic Theory, noted Alfred North Whitehead, "Nature is a dull affair, soundless, scentless, colourless; merely the hurrying of material, endlessly, meaninglessly."[13]

The purpose of science is to unravel mysteries within the physical world. It is not the purpose of science to discover a higher meaning *behind* the physical world or to pretend to 'prove' that no such meaning exists. 'Scientism' begins when the thoughtful respect for science becomes the thoughtless worship of science, and we stop questioning and thinking for ourselves because scientists are supposed to give us the answers to every possible question. Most people think we are now living in an age of science, but we are living in an age of scientism, in which everything, even our thoughts and feelings, are expected to be subject to scientific measurement and scientific analysis. This enormous encroachment of scientific methodology into all aspects of human life and experience, coupled with the spiritually barren assumption that all of Creation can be explained by nineteenth century mechanics, confers a dead, hollow universe. Of course, no one has ever experienced such a universe. The world we experience appears filled with color, fragrance, life and personal choice. Yet, despite this, these fantastic materialist assumptions about what is real and what is not, what is important and what is not, underlie the so-called 'common sense' of most educated contemporary Westerners twenty-four hundred years after Democritus.

As a result, a veiled feeling of *meaninglessness* is a primary characteristic of the contemporary psyche. And this belittling acceptance of ultimate insignificance – which is so completely at odds with the ideals of the Enlightenment and the ideals of the American experiment – provides all the necessary groundwork for selfishness, boredom, hatred, servility, violence and fear. The consequences of meaninglessness are seen throughout that disintegration of human life which is so pitilessly recorded in each day's news report, whether it be cruelty toward oneself, toward other people, toward other creatures, or toward the earth. This would not be able to occur so continuously and so easily if our thoughts, feelings and actions were grounded in the perception of human value and purpose in a living and sacred world. But without this inner perception*, the violence and drug abuse, the racism, pollution, and disease, the rape, hunger, and homelessness, the threat of genetic catastrophe, the threat of nuclear catastrophe, plus all the anger, unhappiness, alienation and cruelty which pervade so much of human life, will automatically continue unrestrained.

These critical problems which confront the human species can never be resolved merely by instituting new governmental policies, furthering economic growth, or awaiting future developments in technological science. Our exaggerated reliance on these external saviors is a symptom of the problem itself. Politics, economics and technology have a valuable place in our lives, but they are only truly valuable when they are ruled by men and women of conscience.

But when conscience succumbs to meaninglessness, values are determined by fleeting fashion and whim, and politics, economics and technology become the rulers, as we become their slaves. Sadly, noted G.I. Gurdjieff, the world requires automatons. "One thing alone is certain, that man's slavery grows and increases. Man is becoming a willing slave. He no longer needs chains. He begins to grow fond of his slavery, to be proud of it. And this is the most terrible thing that can happen to a man."[14]

~

The Modern Age is considered to have begun with the Enlightenment, when medieval religion's oppressive grip on the human mind was relinquished and reason was set free. The real crux of modernism is the belief that we can know

---

* This is not to suggest that orthodox religious belief, blind faith, or a childish reliance on an 'invisible friend in the sky', are necessary precursors of morality. Moral sense and decency are hardly unique to religious believers. In fact, religions often lead to precisely the opposite when they support the destruction of individuality and personal conscience, paradoxically promoting contempt and hatred for much of the beauty, dignity, and diversity of life and creation, rather than encouraging respect, wonder, and delight. That's *real* sacredness.

and understand the universe by applying objective reason to the material world. The knowledge we obtain by this method, called 'science', is Truth. Reason is assumed to be the highest form of human functioning and is therefore the proper judge of what is True, and consequently it is also the proper judge of what is Good (ethics) and what is Beautiful (aesthetics).

This point of view persists today as the prevalent way of thinking in the western world. On the positive side, it has led to magnificent achievements in medicine, technology, industry, agriculture, aeronautics, and communications, to name but a few. On the negative side, it has led to pollution of the environment, weaponry that threatens total annihilation, mindless consumerism, and an empty sense that life on earth is nothing but an insignificant fluke.

Actually, much of the scientific worldview of modernism has been abandoned in recent times by relativistic and quantum science, but it remains deeply ingrained in our psyches and continues to affect all aspects of our daily lives. For instance, our fascination with taking things apart, examining and classifying the pieces, and not carefully considering how to put them back together, applies to our relationships with family and community just as much as to the objects of laboratory study. This way of thinking leads to the fragmentation of our social lives, especially today when technological advancements enable us to leave our homes and roots at a moment's notice and resettle in distant parts of the planet by the end of the day, maintaining superficial relationships with cell phones and computers. Thus the coherence of community decays.

Not that freeing oneself from the confines of a stifling environment is a bad thing, or that the pursuit of individual freedom and personal growth is a bad thing. But there is a vital distinction that is often missed between genuine positive freedom and the unsalvageable destruction of meaningful human connections. When community no longer nourishes, and it becomes necessary to break communal links, *new* human relations must be established. Personal freedom *grows* when the individual is nourished, sustained, and supported by love, when uniqueness is cherished, and communication is warm and plentiful. But freedom corrodes and perishes in the anonymity of standardized mechanical mass culture, where conformity masquerades as equality, and we are free to make whatever life choices we wish to make but have no healthy criteria for making them.

Postmodernism

The movement called 'Postmodernism' began as a reaction against Modernism, brought about by disenchantment with classical science and rationalism, and the kind of civilization these things have wrought. Postmodernism took its cue from the scientific dilemma regarding subjectivity and objectivity that made its appearance in theoretical physics: the classical assumption that it was possible to conduct a purely objective examination of external matter turned out to be untenable. This raised the question of whether external reality *even exists*, or whether it is only an image constructed by a subjective mind. The postmodern answer is that it really does not matter, since it accepts without question that our perceptions are all we can know of reality anyway. This interpretation means in turn that only subjectivity has any actual significance for us, since everything, from matters of taste to religious belief to scientific truth, can be nothing more than personal opinion.*

---

* Since science can no longer be explained as a search for truth about reality (there being no such thing), but is only a matter of personal opinion, the only kind of knowledge that can possibly be of any genuine use is simple, functional 'data' – thus, everything we do in the fields of business or education must now be 'data-driven' to avoid accusations of unprofessionalism or amateurishness. Here is the perfect philosophy for the computer age: unless it is data that can be put into a computer, it is not real knowledge. The opposite of knowledge is no longer ignorance; the opposite of knowledge is "noise" – something unrecognizable (read 'useless') to the machines.

This being so, every opinion must be accorded equal respect, since each opinion is just as subjectively true as any other. (Look at some of the baseless political beliefs that many people today cling to, and the anger and indignation they display if these sacred personal opinions are challenged with facts.) Thus, postmodernists have to maintain a strangely paradoxical absolute faith that nothing is absolute, and they have to be tolerant of anything and everything. Knowledge is demeaned, morality is belittled, and every notion, whether thoughtful or insane, is given equal credence. Relativism (which we will discuss more fully in a later chapter) becomes postmodernism's moral imperative, and this means that postmodernism, like relativism, is morally bankrupt and incoherent. The new twist, however, is that moral bankruptcy and incoherency are not problems anymore! They are just as good as anything else, and we might as well enjoy ourselves and revel in the absurdity. Modern artists often recognized the tragic emptiness that the worldview of positivistic science had spawned, and sought in their art to provide some sense of meaning and comfort. Postmodern artists see exactly the same emptiness, but they do not call it tragic. They are satisfied with the meaninglessness and are eager to make the best of it.

Meanwhile, anyone who disagrees with this analysis, and continues to insist on the possibility that some things besides 'data' might be objectively true, is merely revealing their deep-seated sexist, aristocratic and racist motives. Everything thus becomes political for postmodernists, who are suspicious of anyone claiming to know anything, and intolerant (paradoxically enough) of anything claimed to be true for anyone other than the speaker, and possibly a very small, specific, local environment of listeners.

All civilizations, we are told, have been wrongly based on what postmodernists call 'grand narratives' – comprehensive theories and stories about reality that claim to be necessarily true, and that form the foundation of a society's (not just a small local community's) general beliefs and practices. Greek mythology, the various religions, classical science, stories about America's founding fathers, are all examples of grand narratives. Postmodernism is a critique of grand narratives, attacking them as being essentially little more than festering sexism, racism, and exploitation, full of contradictions, inconsistencies, and lies. One interesting consequence has been the rise of religious fundamentalism as a kind of resistance to the questioning of the grand narratives of religion, and the rise of conservatism as a resistance to the questioning of the grand narratives of politics – hence the two movements become bedfellows (witness the 'religious right' in America today) in their common distaste for postmodernism. On the other hand, the postmodernist willingness to accept anyone's opinion attracts many radicals and liberals. Thus the dualisms return with a vengeance, the arguments get more heated and more vicious, and the rifts just widen even more.

Closely related to and intertwined with postmodernism is the cultural critique called 'deconstructionism'. Originally a method of literary criticism, deconstructionism has been expanded into a strategy for analyzing and interpreting science, philosophy, religion, history, politics, art, and ultimately all aspects of contemporary life. Resembling the reductive method of science, it consists of breaking things down into small fundamental elements that are considered more 'real' than the whole – but in this case, instead of atomic particles, the fundamental elements turn out to be *psychological motives*. By analyzing language, deconstructionists strive to uncover and expose the hidden ideological biases that reveal what the author's words 'really' mean. Any claim that a work of art expresses something noble, true or meaningful, is easily discredited by the analysis of sexist, racist, ethnic, and other base motivations that are unearthed by applying the method. Only small specific details can be accepted as valid, since there are always deceptive political, cultural, or economic assumptions lurking behind any suggestion of a big general truth. Details which the author does *not* include are particularly subject to suspicion: any use of such words as "all men believe", for instance, does not include "all men *and women* believe", and since this clearly indicates sexist inclinations any possible value in the words that follow must automatically be precluded.

Deconstructionism has become the great motivator of our contemporary Press: ignoring the great issues of the day, but indulging in sensational attacks, gossip, and smarmy efforts to discredit all and sundry.

A concern with unearthing and examining motivations certainly has value, but deconstructionism goes way over the top and becomes yet another arrogant absolutism. Thus, the spirit of truth and reason is denied, and our horizons get narrower and narrower. Everything once considered beautiful, meaningful and sublime, whether in art, philosophy or politics, is now subject to being deconstructed and debunked, scientifically reduced to scattered fragments of negative personality traits, deception, and bad faith, exposed as nothing more substantial than a handful of ugly, dangerous and politically incorrect motives. And like scientific reductionism, once something has been deconstructed it most probably cannot be put back together again.

The lazy wish to remain ignorant and apathetic is given the stamp of approval by this phenomenon, since what poets and thinkers actually say or intend is of no importance. If Shakespeare had had the benefits of modern therapy and postmodern philosophy, he would never have had to write Macbeth, so why bother reading it?

In the end, very little is left:

- The only things that are *real* are subjectivity and personal opinion;

- The only things that are *important* are functionality and personal comfort;

- The only things that are *honest and genuine* are our base motivations.

There is no recourse, so we might as well enjoy the absurdity.

At least modernism held out the hope that science would create a better world. Postmodernists view that as hopelessly naïve nonsense.

The great irony is that all this postmodern analysis and psychological cynicism is just an elaborate and pretentious recurrence of ancient Greek sophistry. The Sophists were philosophic teachers who taught that there is no such thing as absolute truth, but only subjective truths that hold for a given person at a given time. Like Socrates, they sought to liberate young minds from uncritical assumptions – they did this by using rhetorical skills to demonstrate that for any rational argument there is always an equally skillful rational *counter*-argument. So far, so good. But unlike Socrates, they stopped here, merely concluding that 'truth' must be relative and subjective – and having wiped out everything that had guided their students' lives and given them meaning, they simply left them empty.

Socrates, on the other hand, showed his young followers that by dropping their unfounded assumptions about what is true, they arrived at the *beginning* of their quest for wisdom and meaning. Postmodernists, like the sophists, are already finished. Spiritual emptiness and intellectual collapse are the end of the road. Just add a little modern self-centeredness and a hefty dose of political correctness, and ancient Greek sophistry becomes postmodernism.

Postmodern philosophers took up the challenge when contemporary science began questioning our fundamental assumptions about objectivity, perception, and reason. But rather than acknowledging the shortcomings of reason and searching for something higher, they merely maintained that *nothing* is higher, nothing matters, and nothing is worth longing for.

They shrank before the threshold that might have reopened the door to transcendence.

CHAPTER TWO

A MEANINGFUL EDUCATION

Millions of Americans have been persuaded that the only purpose of education is to prepare our children to score well on standardized tests so we can have more well-trained workers. As the standards movement bludgeons along, we convince ourselves that being a useful employee is the only key to a happy and successful life. Rather than nurturing a sense of wonder, respect for wisdom, and a passion for learning, our schools are thus increasingly devoted to standardizing knowledge into lists of data, telling students what is appropriate for them to know and think, and then 'scientifically' measuring how well they can regurgitate this data on assessment tests.

What is truly important in human life consists precisely of those things that cannot be measured; love, decency, joy, all the great virtues and passions. This is what the education of a human being should be about. But America no longer seeks to educate thinking, feeling, human beings. We seek to educate servants. We all know that the rallying cry 'Raising Standards' is just a euphemism for job training and an excuse for a bit of cynical union-busting.

All of this is a prescription for an efficient human ant hill. It is worth remembering that in the ant hill an individual life does not count for much: there are always plenty of replacements who can do the same job. In a misguided effort to lift everyone up, we lower our expectations for a vibrant and meaningful life and then *homogenize* everyone. This quickly becomes a methodical program for obliterating individuality and *joie de vivre,* masquerading as concern for our children's future.

The corporate world gets involved in education, worried that their businesses will not be able to compete in the global economy if the workers being produced by our schools are inferior. They then insist that schools should be run like any other enterprise in a competitive marketplace, and the rules of quality control, managerial efficiency, and good marketing technique, should be applied in exactly the same way. Thus, we need (1) a common set of standards for the end-product, (2) a scientific test for measuring how well the students and schools are meeting these standards, and (3) an advertising campaign to convince the trusting public that a meaningful education of their children means getting them to score well on these tests. This latter is easily achieved by appealing to parents' worries about the financial future, and then ceaselessly sending them the message that our schools are in a 'crisis'.

But the economic system is not floundering because of badly performing schools. The American economy rises and falls, as it does in every nation and in every era, in response to numerous and profound market and social forces that bear no relation at all to the day-to-day functioning of our educational system. Meanwhile, the insistence on greater 'accountability' of schools does not lead to greater achievement by our students. It leads to greater stress, fear, and alienation, it leads to a dumbing-down of curricula, it leads to pain and stigmatization for many children who do not do well on standardized tests regardless of their intelligence or classroom efforts, and it helps to deepen the rifts between diverse and antagonistic elements of society.

This certainly does not mean that there is no room for improvement in the school system. On the contrary, it has ceased to surprise me, but continues to sadden me, when after all the talk about 'raising standards' another group of fresh young faces enters a college class I am teaching, and they do not know how to add two fractions together or how to do other things they should have mastered long ago. Clearly, something needs to change. But narrowing our vision and stultifying our minds is not a very useful or admirable reform, and it is merely degrading and destructive to base our educational system on a corporate model, treating our children as nothing more than future workers and consumers who are to be counted, measured, and evaluated.

Americans are used to the entrenched system of educational experts using test scores to label us as smart or not smart, worthy or not worthy, even though such tests clearly have little ability to predict either academic or worldly success: rather, the scores tend to be highly correlated with socioeconomic status, and they reward the superficial learning of meaningless rote data rather than critical thinking, creativity, or depth of understanding. Of course, it is worth remembering that the ideal citizen of a politically corrupt state or an oligarchic state is a gullible fool. An educated, well-informed citizenry is required for democracy to function appropriately, since such people are more difficult to lie to and are less likely to believe all the delusions and misinformation that can be spread on the internet or cable TV. As Jefferson warned us, "If a nation expects to be ignorant and free, in a state of civilization, it expects what never was and never will be."

There is more than ample evidence that these costly examinations tell us little about intelligence or competency – which is why, e.g., more and more colleges and universities have been dropping the requirement that all applicants take the SAT's. Colleges know that these standard assessments merely measure one's ability to do well *on the test*, a worthless skill in the long run.* But even though public school test scores have remained virtually unchanged since 1971, the general public continues to believe the propaganda

---

* When I was 40 years old, I decided to go back to school and study law. In order to get into a good law school, I knew it would be necessary to do well on a standardized test, the LSAT, that all prospective law students had to take. So six weeks before the test date I joined a 'Test Prep' course. The first night of the class, I took a sample LSAT (a released test from a previous year) and I scored in what would have been the 70th percentile. Six weeks later, after working very hard to prepare myself, I took the test for real and scored in the 98th percentile. I was no smarter than I had been six weeks earlier. I was no better educated. I just knew how to take this particular test.

that the tests are important indicators of the quality of our schools. The result is the further stratification of society along racial* and economic lines, and the further erosion of our individuality.

Cultivating an ever-deepening sense of wonder, nurturing a wide-eyed longing for wisdom, meaning, and completeness: this is the true function of education. But this has all been deconstructed and debunked, and we have deprived our children of the opportunity to take mystery seriously, or to enjoy the challenge of 'not knowing' and the excitement of a new discovery. Our complacent acceptance of cultural directives that tell us what to think and feel has opened the way for the mass degradation of America's children by subjecting them to 'scientific measurements', as if they were soulless mechanical devices that need to be repaired and upgraded. Our schools have thus been forced into the business of cloning mediocrity, churning out obedient workers for the economic system, who will not rock the status quo.

But our schools are not in a 'crisis'. It is our souls that are in peril.

Moral and Intellectual Inferiority

This whole idea of testing the intellect began with the Eugenics Movement in the early twentieth century. 'Intelligence Tests' were originally concocted as tools for demonstrating the moral and intellectual inferiority of

---

* Public schools, especially those in affluent neighborhoods, now have incentives to resist accepting students with educational deficiencies, since they will bring down the scores: lowered scores lead to schools being labeled as 'failures', which means that reputations are ruined and jobs are lost. From this perspective, it is better for the schools if these children drop out. Or perhaps they can be referred to a commercially run 'Job Corps' for a GED, where the corporate degradation of education reaches the extreme of absurdity. In a Job Corps where I once briefly worked, the students – living, human children, most of whom were Black or Hispanic and came from inner city communities – were officially referred to at our staff meetings as 'the inventory'. No lie.

immigrants, Blacks, Jews, Native Americans, etc. "The nation's pioneers of intelligence tests provided lawmakers with the scientific rationale they needed for policies that are now roundly condemned....Tens of thousands of army recruits, including recent immigrants, were subjected to IQ tests; bizarre but supposedly scientific conclusions about the natural laws of intelligence were drawn; and eugenically appropriate public policies were enacted in several states."[15] All of this was expected to be useful toward the goal of selecting better people to become citizens, "and even for the right of having offspring," as one of the founders of the movement wrote in 1927.[16]

According to Lewis M. Terman of Stanford University, the developer of the Stanford-Binet Intelligence Scale:

> It is safe to predict that in the near future intelligence tests will bring tens of thousands of these high-grade defectives under the surveillance and protection of society. This will ultimately result in curtailing the reproduction of feeblemindedness....[17]

Here was faith in mechanical science gone mad. Today we have altered the language, of course. We no longer speak of 'social defectives', 'morons' and 'imbeciles'. We speak instead of people who have 'special needs', or any number of 'learning disabilities'. But the game is the same – the worthy are separated off from the unworthy. "The eugenics movement may have faltered," notes Peter Sacks, "but it nevertheless formed certain habits of mind that have been institutionalized in the American belief system."[18] These habits of thought continue to exacerbate the wide differences between socioeconomic groups.

This is not meant to suggest some sort of evil conspiracy, consciously spawned by a depraved cabal bent on reducing men and women into sheep. Rather, it represents an unconscious cultural trend that persists by its own overwhelming inertia, and will continue to lead us into the appalling degradation of the human ant hill if we as individuals continue to passively submit to it.

The development of these mental tests coincided perfectly with the needs of the newly emergent American middle class. The question of how to devise new rules for allocating wealth based on merit rather than ancestry (an excellent project) found its answer in the modern world's fascination with science and technology. Measuring minds with technology, and using this information to assess merit, seemed an ideal solution. The old aristocracy used to perpetuate itself on the basis of birth and parentage. Now the new elites could perpetuate their class privilege with tests legitimized by pseudo-science.

This is an example of the ideal of freedom finding itself at odds with the ideal of equality (a tension, I hasten to add, which the founders of the United States very carefully, wisely, and deliberately crafted). 'Freedom' demands that all citizens have the right to a successful life, regardless of the circumstances of their birth, if they work hard and do their best. Unfortunately, it is now assumed (conveniently but with scant evidence) that standardized tests of intelligence are a valid scientific way of guaranteeing this freedom, by assigning people to their proper place within the meritocracy. 'Equality', the standard-bearer for fairness, justice and a level playing-field for all, then asserts itself in *opposition* to this economic hierarchy that distinguishes one person from another rather than making everyone equal. So the rules of Equal Protection come into force to balance out the situation, by insisting on new requirements of 'inclusion' in the classroom and 'accommodations' during testing for all children with 'special needs'. (Unsurprisingly, the number of kids diagnosed with 'special needs' has grown exponentially in the years since the standards movement began, a huge boon for the pharmaceutical industry.) The final result is that almost everyone graduates from high school anyway, so the assessment tests become little more than an expensive annoyance, creating bureaucratic jobs while distressing students and debasing their education.*

The remaining claim that the tests cause schools to raise standards is also untrue. Just the reverse usually occurs: a 'dumbing down' is the inevitable result when community and political pressures force schools and teachers to restrict teaching time to details and question-types that are most likely to appear on the standardized tests. Creativity, innovation, imagination, and in-depth thinking, are all relegated to the category of 'fluff' so that children's minds can be focused exclusively on test details. Schools should be helping our children become happy, moral, responsible citizens who care about their families, their communities, their country and the world. Art, music, drama and athletics are just as important for the development of mature, well-rounded adults as English, science, history and math.

Of course, there are ways that schools can succeed in raising test scores, and many have done so. Deprive our children of recess and athletics (probably the most important aspect of education for young children who are developing physically), eliminate art and music (probably the most important aspect of education for adolescents who are developing emotionally), forego time for interesting discussions, offer less time to read books for pleasure, cut back on field trips and interesting projects, offer fewer electives, and waste a lot of valuable time teaching test-taking tricks, and it is fairly easy to raise scores. But the results are meaningless at best. At worst, they numb our children's minds, narrow their vision, and kill their spirit, by turning education into a boring, frightening, drudgery. Recently there have even been calls for the elimination of

---

* Relying on the American ideal of 'freedom' as a justification for testing intelligence and divvying people into a meritocracy, is a conservative project concerned with maintaining a healthy economy. Relying on the corresponding American ideal of 'equality' as a justification for rules and regulations that ensure fair treatment of everyone, is a liberal project concerned with maintaining social justice. There is certainly nothing wrong with either of these concerns, but neither endeavor is primarily concerned with the education of children.

childhood summer vacations, since ten weeks of fun and fresh air get in the way of preparing for the tests and threaten our position in the global marketplace. Meanwhile, we find ourselves callously falling into a hellish and caricaturish world in which more and more high school students respond to the pressures of college admission by contemplating suicide, elementary school children become ill and obese from lack of recess and play, and kindergartners require therapy to recover from stress disorders. If we notice children getting restless after making them sit still for hours doing as they are told, rather than saying "Why don't you get up and go play," we say, "We had better get you tested, you may need medication."

To reform our schools in a meaningful way would mean to restore the notion that education is rooted in wonder, not economics. Wonder is not merely curiosity. It is a blending of enchantment, mystery, love and respect, with thoughtfulness, openness, trust, and intuition. It reveals to us the intimate relationship between our inner selves and the outer world. But as we have noted, an outmoded but persistent scientific viewpoint has led us to take the self *out* of life. We insist on remaining disconnected onlookers, believing that 'real' life only exists in external things, and our 'real' need is to accumulate more of them. In addition to devastating our souls, this has utterly crippled our educational system. Like bits of matter in a laboratory or human beings in a community, it is a fiction to believe that knowledge and ideas can be isolated and objectively measured. They grow, develop and change as they pass through time, they are intertwined with other ideas and interwoven with subjective hearts and minds. Knowledge, intelligence and ideas are not scientifically reducible 'things'. And neither are our children. Children are not meant to be assessed like commercial products on an assembly line. Schools should not be in the business of manufacturing 'things'.

But since the light of meaning has dimmed, and our remaining purpose in life is to be a conforming worker ant for forty to sixty hours per week and then watch advertisements and go shopping during the time remaining, there is little time and even less need for actual thinking in any sort of active, creative, or meaningful way. Public opinion, represented by our polling madness which tells us what our opinions are, has conveniently spared us any need to think intelligently for ourselves, by giving us an opportunity to accommodate our beliefs to the prevailing nonsense before we open our mouths and embarrass ourselves. And if we do not have to think for ourselves, if we do not have or respect our own minds, then one can only conclude that an empty education that strives for bland uniformity of thinking is both natural and obvious.

A major concern of education should be to create an atmosphere of trust where radical questioning is encouraged, where children feel free to fearlessly express their insights and find answers to their own questions. Openness to ideas and possibilities, an expanded vision, a willingness to explore, a passion for discovery, a genuine appreciation for wisdom and beauty, and a full life of the emotions, mind, body and spirit – these should be the goals of our educational endeavor. Planning lessons is a useful tool for teachers: reflecting on content, comparing alternative ways of approaching the material, considering possible questions that might arise. But forcing teachers to rigidly adhere to pre-planned 'objectives' and specific measurements of 'learning outcomes' has the effect of forcing teachers to be insensitive to where children are at that moment, to shun innovation, and to impatiently close down questioning. *Good* teachers know that the classroom, like the rest of life, rarely sticks to the plan, and teaching requires improvisation, sensitivity, and countless unexpected turns. *Great* teachers use this unpredictability to unlock minds and confound expectations: if Socrates had focused on achieving measurable pre-planned objectives, his Teachings would have been meaningless and quickly forgotten. But under pressure from school boards, politicians, and bureaucratic regulators (who typically know nothing about the classroom) to specify 'learning objectives' and 'means of assessing outcomes' – that is, to isolate and name in advance specific behavioral (scientifically measurable) goals – teaching becomes a mere dead mechanical transfer of data. But education is not the passing of information from someone who has it to someone who does not. That is called 'programming'.

Yet that is precisely what we blindly pretend is happening when we give our children great arrays of "pre-tests" and "benchmark tests" to find out exactly what it is they know and what they do not know, and then devise "strategies" that are "data driven" by "statistics" to fill in what is missing inside their brains. This is all a farce. It neatly compartmentalizes everyone and everything in the schools, and it allows for lots of forms to be filled out and filed in the appropriate drawers and sent to the appropriate government agencies. But children are not machines that can simply be turned on and off whenever we want them to regurgitate uniform answers to questions on cue, and they typically do not take pre-tests seriously anyway ("This don't count," they say, "so why should I spend time working out this math problem? I'll do it when we take the *real* test" – and while this kind of self-confidence is not always realistic, it quite often is). So the "data" is merely a pretense, it is not really accurate, sensible or useful, and the only thing it "drives" is a lot of wasted class time going over things that many kids know already, and those that do not usually need something far more important than simply repeating the same prescribed lesson plan at them over and over again, no matter how many diverse 'teaching styles', 'strategies', and canned techniques-of-the-day are dragged into the classroom by the latest wave of 'experts'.

The Lost Longing

Young students are obsessed with the questions: "Why do I need to know this? When am I ever going to use this in my real life?" Since they have almost never heard that inner development and inner wisdom are important, that their inner dreams and aspirations *are* their 'real' life, this kind of dry utilitarianism is all that makes sense to them. They want to be assured that the only things they are being taught are things that will help assure them of a good job. Otherwise, or so they believe without question, they have more important things to do. And as far as their vision allows them to see, adult society agrees with them. Thus, we reduce life to a base minimum.

Among animals, puberty is the pinnacle of maturity. There is nothing to be accomplished after that. Among humans, however, puberty is just the beginning of adulthood. The greater and most interesting part of learning – emotional, intellectual, moral, and spiritual – follows afterward. But we customarily think that we, like the animals, have nothing much to learn after puberty, other than a few last-minute details that will hopefully help us land a good job. We are all finished with wonder by the age of fourteen. After that, we train to become competent workers or specialists, but otherwise do not grow or change very much. We are content with mediocrity, and smile with a mixture of bemusement and embarrassment at any mention of our naïve childhood hopes and dreams.

Given the smug arrogance they witness in our 'scientific' society, it is not surprising that kids simply do not know that real intelligence means openness – not the current vogue that any silly opinion must be granted the same respect as any other, but real openness to ambiguity, possibility and wonder, an attitude toward life that combines genuine common sense with the innocence of a child, that does not grovel before the hypnotic enslaving effects of cultural propaganda and fads, or revel in the teenage passions for ignorance, vulgarity, and boredom.

Part of the explanation for the current situation is that our schools are now scrutinized as if they were totally responsible for the success of their students – as if parents and the kids themselves bear hardly any responsibility. The result is that a substantial number of children come swaggering into the classroom having no reason to be polite or respectful, and no incentive to make any serious effort. It is the teacher who must be endlessly patient and tolerant of their behavior, and prove his or her own worth to parents and school boards by coaxing, cajoling and begging the students to study and do well on the tests. Children today have been led to believe that they deserve a great deal of respect, and they are adamant that no one be allowed to 'dis' them. But many of them have never been taught that they must *earn* this respect by making serious efforts of their own. With the best of intentions, we have tried so hard to imbue them superficially with self-esteem that we have crippled their ability to accomplish anything on their own. And so, instead of studying and working hard and taking any interest in learning and becoming the best that they can be, far too many of them sit in their classrooms passively, talking with each other, listening to music on their headphones, and at semester's end expect a good grade and a good test score. If these do not occur, teachers and administrators are readily blamed. They then take all these attitudes and expectations with them into adulthood, always blaming others for their circumstances.

This opens up the question of why we educate our children to begin with. A few years ago, at yet another of the endless 'professional development trainings' I was attending when I was a high school teacher, we were asked at the end of a session if we had any questions. This is the one I asked: *Why do we do this?* Everyone just laughed, assuming I was being funny – after all, who would ask 'why' we send our kids to school? But I wasn't joking. I think we need to have this discussion big time. Maybe we have no good reason at all, maybe it's just an obsolete holdover from agrarian days: then close the schools! If there *is* a reason, and we agree on what it is, *then* we can make intelligent decisions about how to proceed. But we just keep doing things out of inertia, unwilling to question ourselves at an important fundamental level. If you don't know why you're doing something, how can you know if you're doing it well? How can you make improvements? Personally, I think if we were honest we would notice that we are no longer interested in educating our children to be wise, happy, intelligent citizens and human beings. We are educating them to be cogs in the economic machine. If that's all it's for, let's admit it and get on with it. Why waste money and time on art, music and creative writing? But if that's *not* the reason, or we wish to re-assess the reason, then let's do *that* and get corporate America and government bureaucrats out of the classroom.

The idea of corporatizing schools, like the privatization of the prison system[*], is dangerous, damaging, and outright ludicrous. The reason is obvious: for-profit schools are obliged to care more about their profits than about our children – and no, "the market" will not correct for this bias. This holds true as well for the corporations that provide standardized tests, test preparation books and software, pre-packaged lesson plans for teachers, etc. These companies are making a killing. The purpose of reform is supposed to be to make the world a better place, not to bully and fire people, and dismantle public services, all in the name of private gain. (Unions, on the other hand, which these corporate entities and their political lackeys love to vilify, *improve* the schools, just as they improve working conditions everywhere. Unions

---

[*] Cost-cutting measures at privatized prisons, as required for the financial benefit of investors, have led to insufficient staff, poorly trained staff (hence an increase in reports of abuse), poor healthcare (hence an increase in inmate deaths), far less attention to rehabilitation or counseling (which increases recidivism), etc. This does not serve or protect the public. In fact, it accomplishes precisely the opposite. The reason corporations want in on this action is the disgraceful fact that imprisoning citizens is one of the things America now does better than any other country – one out of every 100 citizens, an 8-fold increase since the 1970's, are in cages: a $3 billion industry. Half are drug offenders (needless to say there's been no lessening of drug abuse). Despite the fact that blacks and whites have roughly identical percentages of illicit drug usage, ten times more prisoners are black. The entire system is a phenomenal example of greed, racism, cruelty, ignorance and ineffectiveness. (ALEC, an odious threat to democracy, lobbies for privatization of prisons as well as schools. They simultaneously promote bills to lengthen sentences while promoting efforts to privatize prisons. See https://www.youtube.com/watch?v=-ISLRYKRCE0 and https://www.youtube.com/watch?v=IyTU9RbOEJo to learn more.)

reduce incentives for teachers to give high grades just to make everyone happy, or to teach to the test. Unions ensure professional training opportunities that are at least *intended* to benefit the *kids*, not the corporations. It is true that unions may sometimes make it difficult to get rid of a genuinely poor teacher, but they also prevent favoritism and cronyism by making promotions and salaries dependent on experience. Anyway, it is arbitrary and ludicrous (and a recent court case corroborates this*) to think that student standardized test scores are an appropriate way to determine the value of a teacher.

Lastly, let me take a moment to note that there is nothing magical about the age of eighteen, and there is no good reason to keep forcing the same testing and programming down the throats of every child, at the same time, in the same way. Some of our children, who are languishing in high school, suffering miserably and distracting their peers, should have the nearly-vanished option of attending a vocational school and learning a trade: precalculus and ancient history are simply not interesting to them, and why must they be? Others are ready well *before* the age of eighteen to enter a community college, and some kids, bored out of their minds, are ready at sixteen or seventeen to enter an early liberal arts college (I am referring to colleges where all or many of the students are young, like Simon's Rock College in Great Barrington, MA, not placing the occasional sixteen-year-old into classrooms filled with nineteen-year-olds). Some would benefit enormously from entering the Service, or leaving school for now without any 'drop out' stigma or repercussions, and getting a job: if these kids later decided they *wanted* to return to high school – mature and ready to succeed – they should be welcome with joy and

---

* Sheri G. Lederman (Plaintiff) v. John B. King, Jr. Commissioner, New York State Education Department, Candace H. Shyer, Assistant Commissioner, Office Of State Assessment of the New York State Education Department (Defendants); Supreme Court of the State of New York, County of Albany.

open arms to schools that could easily accommodate them with evening and weekend class schedules – which could have the added benefit of opening up the facilities for sports, art, lectures and meetings, adult education, coffee houses, concerts, and other community activities. Schools could then become vibrant centers of civic life. (Clearly, there are economic obstacles to such a suggestion, but rather than listing all the dreary reasons why it can't be done, why not find creative ways to do it?)

~

In Socrates' time, youngsters flocked to him, aching to share in his wisdom, wanting to be challenged and taught. Crowds of disciples followed Christ everywhere, so that sometimes he had to get on a boat and sail away, just to find a brief respite.

Why do we have no such ache?

Or do we, but we have nearly deadened it with what we now call 'education'. Is the passionate desire for all that is truly good and meaningful completely dead in ourselves and our children? Or is it just too hard to brave the ridicule of acknowledging that the love of learning, seeking, and striving, still lives on, hidden somewhere deep inside our crust-encovered hearts?

CHAPTER THREE

EMERSON: "I MUST BE MYSELF"

Born in 1803 in Boston, Ralph Waldo Emerson was a great intellect, at a time when a great intellect was still respected in America.[*] He enrolled at Harvard at the age of 14 and later attended Harvard Divinity College, becoming a Unitarian minister. After resigning his pastoral post for doctrinal reasons, he travelled to Europe where he met Carlyle, Coleridge and Wordsworth. In 1836, after returning to America, he published *Nature*, which set down the principles of the philosophy of Transcendentalism.

In addition to Emerson, the Transcendentalists included Henry David Thoreau, Margaret Fuller, Amos Bronson Alcott and his daughter, Louisa May Alcott, and the movement influenced many non-members including Herman Melville, Edgar Allan Poe, and Walt Whitman. The Transcendentalists criticized their contemporary society for its unthinking conformity, and stressed unity with nature, the sanctity of the individual, the efficacy of human striving, and the need to live in the present. They emphasized creativity, imagination, and intuiting higher levels of life beyond what can be seen, heard, or touched, in order to transcend our limitations and discover our true genius. By the 1850's the movement included an increasingly urgent critique of American slavery as well as progressive stands on women's rights and education. (In her famous book, *Little Women*, Louisa May Alcott wrote in 1868, "I believe that it is as much a right and duty for women to do something with their

---

[*] Regrettably, Richard Hofstadter's observation from fifty years ago has only become more true with the passage of time: "...ours is the only educational system in the world, vital segments of which have fallen into hands of people who joyfully and militantly proclaim their hostility to intellect." (*Anti-Intellectualism in American Life,* 1963)

lives as for men and we are not going to be satisfied with such frivolous parts as you give us".)

The reason we ascribe human greatness to certain historical figures, according to Emerson (he mentions Plato, Moses, and John Milton as examples), is that they did not merely tell us what others have thought or written, but spoke their *own* truths and had the courage of their convictions. Each one of us, he suggests, should also "learn to detect and watch that gleam of light"[19] that flashes across our minds from within. But sadly, while listening sheepishly to what others tell us to think and believe, we tend to ignore or dismiss our own deepest ideas and ideals, as if nothing we personally come up with could possibly be all that important.

At some point in our lives, most people will come to the realization that envy is a worthless, foolish emotion. Living our lives in envy or imitation of someone else means that we have effectively given up our *own* life – Emerson calls this psychological suicide. For better or worse, one has only oneself. This is often thought of as a dreary realization, but what it actually tells us is that we are, each one of us, utterly unique. We each have the power, and the *sole* power, to sculpt our own life. "The power which resides in him is new in nature," Emerson wrote, "and none but he knows what that is which he can do." Nor does *he himself* know "until he has tried."

When we forget this, when the influences of contemporary culture and education destroy the awareness of our individual uniqueness, we become "ashamed of that divine idea which each of us represents," and through a kind of spiritual cowardice we shrink from living up to our own deepest truths and aspirations. We feel strong and fulfilled when we really put our heart into something that is important to *us* and we do our best, but most of the time that is not how we live: instead, we belittle ourselves, and our lives become constricted, boring and empty. "It is our light," notes Marianne Williamson in this same vein, "not our darkness that most frightens us. We ask ourselves, Who am I to be brilliant, gorgeous, talented, fabulous? Actually, who are

54

you not to be? You are a child of God. Your playing small does not serve the world. There is nothing enlightened about shrinking so that other people won't feel insecure around you. We are all meant to shine...."[20] Or in Teilhard de Chardin's words, "Our duty, as men and women is to proceed as if limits to our ability did not exist. We are collaborators in creation."[21]

Teilhard's dictum is in line with the Biblical statement that we are made in the image of God. Thus, to a very great extent, we write our own story, our inner thoughts and feelings create our own reality. This means that we are responsible for ourselves, yet it also means our possibilities are endless. If you don't like the story you are hearing, if you don't like the song that you hear all day long in your head, you can sing a different one.

~

Socrates said, "Know thyself." Emerson added, "Trust thyself." Accept what is best and highest within oneself and go forward to meet one's destiny head-on, rather than fleeing from the difficulties of life. This requires confidence and courage. We can take a lesson here from youth. As teenagers, we have a tendency to be brash, impatient and presumptuous, never fretting over consequences, judging things and people quickly on their apparent merits. "This world demands the qualities of youth," noted Robert Kennedy, "not a time of life but a state of mind, a temper of the will, a quality of the imagination, a predominance of courage over timidity, of the appetite for adventure over the life of ease."[22] This is the appropriate attitude of human nature. As adults we become wiser and more careful, but also more timid and fearful: we hold ourselves back from stating our truths openly and defiantly, and we are hesitant to act with courage or joy, mostly because we are trapped by our concern for what others might think. The whole world seems to wag its finger and warn us against independence and individuality. To maintain the peace, we submit to conformity and become averse to self-reliance, averse to discovering or acknowledging who and what we really are.*

We know that when others tell us what is good and true, their words must always be questioned. We pay lip service to this admonition, but it requires more. The integrity of our own mind *must be considered sacred.* "I am ashamed," Emerson lamented, "to think how easily we capitulate to badges and names, to large societies and dead institutions." This does not mean we should stick blindly and stubbornly to every unexamined belief. Most of the time, 'belief' is only a way of adhering to one conviction or another on thoughtless and inadequate grounds: perhaps because someone told us to believe it, perhaps because believing it makes us comfortable and spares us the effort of thinking for ourselves. Emerson is speaking here of an inner certainty that is not based on submissiveness to others, mere stubbornness, or wishful thinking, but on *objective inner experience.* I remember along these lines an evening long ago when a wise teacher of mine made a statement and asked me what I thought of what he had claimed. I said politely, "I believe you." Boy, was *that* ever the wrong answer! He bellowed at me so that the room shook, "You believe me?!? You have *no right* to believe what I say! How *dare* you take my work for your own! You find out for *yourself!"*

Emerson grieved over the fact that we all tend to be far too concerned with how we look in others people's eyes. This is why we often do what we think we *ought* to do – which means that even if it *is* what we ought to do *this is the wrong reason for doing it.* "Men do what is called a good action," he bemoaned, such as "some piece of courage or charity, much as they would pay a fine…. Their works are done as an apology…. Their virtues are penances." This is simply hypocrisy – acts of kindness and generosity that have

---

* "The greatest error of a man is to think that he is weak by nature, evil by nature. Every man is divine and strong in his real nature. What are weak and evil are his habits, his desires and thoughts, but not himself."
– Ramana Maharshi

nothing to do with one's own volition. "I do not wish to expiate, but to live."

Plato spoke of this same hypocrisy in the *Symposium*. There, the character of Phaedrus calls Love "a mighty god", and he says that of all the gods Love is the most beneficial to man. This, he says, is because the principle which ought to govern a person's life is a sense of honor (for without honor people would never accomplish any great deeds) and a lover who is caught in a dishonorable act by the beloved will be utterly humiliated. The fear of this embarrassment, and the pride we feel when our lover sees us acting well, provide the motivating force that can lead us to acts of greatness, and this is all thanks to Love.

Phaedrus' reasons for honoring the god of Love, of course, are derived solely from his concern with appearances. He finds love useful because by making us worry about how we appear to others we are induced to act honorably, or even nobly, out of some combination of fear, shame, or pride. In this negative and rather depressing way, Love coerces people to behave 'as if' they were virtuous. But Emerson states (and Plato would agree), "My life is for itself and not for a spectacle."

It is difficult to stick to the principle that our thoughts and actions should not be based on what other people think. But this is a difference between greatness of soul and meagerness of soul. It is all the harder, Emerson acknowledges, "because you will always find those who think they know what is your duty better than you know it." As a consequence, it is always easiest to live in accord with other people's opinions and wishes. At the other extreme, it is also fairly easy to think and act from one's own self *if* one *withdraws from active life* and lives in complete solitude. But a truly great man or woman is the one "who in the midst of the crowd" maintains their independence and individuality.

Another concern that destroys self-trust is our fear of appearing inconsistent, since the only way people know us is through our past acts and words, and we worry about disappointing them. But this keeps us always looking backwards. Why drag along dead thoughts and beliefs, just to make sure we never contradict something we have said in the past? What is so terrible about contradicting oneself? This just prevents us from ever learning anything new.

> A foolish consistency is the hobgoblin of little minds, adored by little statesmen and philosophers and divines. With consistency a great soul has simply nothing to do.... Is it so bad, then, to be misunderstood? Pythagoras was misunderstood, and Socrates, and Jesus, and Luther, and Copernicus, and Galileo, and Newton, and every pure and wise spirit that ever took flesh. To be great is to be misunderstood.

So Emerson hoped to hear no more about conformity and consistency, two words he felt should be relegated to the category of the ridiculous. Enough, then, of mediocrity and contentment, enough of skulking and fear: "Let us never bow and apologize more."

In one of my favorite poems, the great Rumi wrote:

> *When you feel the qualities of Gabriel in you,*
> *you fly up quickly*
> *like a fledgling not thinking of the ground.*
> *When you feel asinine qualities in you,*
> *no matter how hard you try to do otherwise,*
> *you will head toward the stable.*

> *The mouse is not despicable for its form,*
> *which is a helpless victim to birds of prey,*
> *the mouse who loves dark places and cheese*
> *and pistachio nuts and syrup.*
> *But when the white falcon*
> *has the inner nature of a mouse*
> *it is a disgrace to all animals.*[23]

All too often, we behave like the donkey and tamely head to the stable, always begging, and fawning, and flattering the influential, in order to gain approval or advantage.

But suppose, for a moment, that we lift ourselves up and begin to "feel the qualities of Gabriel" inside ourselves. If we "trust ourselves", what is it that is being trusted? What do these words actually mean? *What is the nature of this 'self' on which our trust is supposed to rely?*

It is an inner living 'something' that says "I Am". It is the primary existential instinct that arises deep within our consciousness. We share this inner 'something' with all of life – it is the same source from which everything proceeds. "We first share the life by which things exist," Emerson states, "and [only] afterwards see them as appearances in nature, and forget that we have shared their cause." This shared living essence, he says, this elemental place within us that is One with all existence, is the "fountain of action and of thought." This is the source of human genius, the ground of spontaneous intuition, the root of inspiration. "In that deep force, the last fact behind which analysis cannot go, all things find their common origin." It is *this* that we must learn to trust.

But it needs to be understood that this is not our 'ego', it is not our 'personality' or our ordinary sense of self.[*] It is something much more. It is a hidden place within our mind that *absolutely knows*, beyond any mere opinion, the difference between right and wrong, the difference between lies and truth. It is what Plato called *Nous*, the 'eye of the soul'. (Other traditions call it 'the third eye'. In the Gospels, Christ refers to the consciousness of *Nous* in Matthew 6:22 when he says, "The light of the body is the eye: if therefore thine eye be single, thy whole body shall be full of light.")

---

[*] "Whoever wants the 'I' to yield up its mysterious and tremendous secret must stop it from looking perpetually in the mirror, must stop the little ego's fascination with its own image." – Paul Brunton, *The Notebooks of Paul Brunton*

Nous is that special place in our intellect that arrives at knowledge by sudden, uncontradictable, *insight*. Such an insight (we have all had them) may follow in the wake of a long and painstaking period of questioning and pondering, or it may appear inexplicably out of the blue, but when it arrives it arrives in a flash. In general, these are rare and involuntary events, for this is a potential human faculty that usually lies dormant as we meander through our day-to-day lives. But Socrates believed that it is possible for this faculty to become conscious and deliberate. In fact, he taught that awakening *Nous,* opening the eye – not merely studying or thinking – is the highest task of anyone who wishes to perfect his or her soul. It is possible, even easy, to have a keen and clever mind, to know a great many facts, and to be filled with practical and theoretical knowledge, and yet to have no authentic Wisdom because one's *Nous* has never awakened. Such a soul is like a ship whose rightful captain has been overthrown, a ship that is either in a state of endless anarchy, or which has been taken over by one or another tyrannical usurper: some harsh or foolish passion, appetite, belief or prejudice that rules and effectively ruins one's life.

For Socrates, wisdom is not about knowing many things or understanding difficult ideas. It is always and only about awakening one's soul to wonder and insight.

> Plato refers to *Nous* as the eye of the soul. *Nous* is that which "sees" into the nature of essential meanings and values. To have an awakened *Nous* is to be led by an inner eye of the soul which others lack, no matter how intelligent or well informed they might be.[24]

This means, in Emerson's words, that we "lie in the lap of immense intelligence, which makes us receivers of its truth and organs of its activity." We have only to awaken to it. When we discern justice, when we discern truth, "we do nothing of ourselves." We simply allow these realizations, which are already within us, to enter our conscious awareness.[*] We can all distinguish our usual chattering thoughts from these deeper spontaneous intuitions. We may not be able to articulate the latter, but we know "these things are so, like day and night, not to be disputed."

But we are programmed by our environment and education to mistrust our intuition – to mistrust, in fact, anything we cannot measure or touch. *Nous* frightens and threatens our narrow little ego, challenging its total power over our lives. The self-defensive response is to put up a kind of psychological 'wall' that stops us from perceiving such things, so we forget about them and go back to our comfortable, unimaginative, pre-programmed lives. Thus:

> Man is timid and apologetic; he is
> no longer upright; he dares not say
> 'I think,' 'I am,' but quotes some
> saint or sage.

Perhaps it is more timely to say that in our epoch, because we find so little of interest or value within ourselves, we fill our time with gossip about celebrities and *that* is who we quote.

Instead of living in the present ("I am"), we look backward and lament the past, or forward into an imaginary future, but either way we are "heedless of the riches" that surround us *right now*. We do not hear our own authentic voice, or if we manage to hear it we do not trust it, but only listen attentively to the surface voice of others.

In religion, perhaps most markedly, we are expected to accept external teachings as facts that we must believe. I have always found it fascinating, and disheartening, that very few people seem to notice that in that climactic moment in the New Testament, when Pilate asks Jesus, "Are you the

---

[*] "The problem in our society and in our schools," wrote Joseph Campbell in *Thou Art That*, "is to inculcate, without overdoing it, the notion of education, as in the Latin 'educere'—to lead, to bring out what is in someone rather than merely to indoctrinate him/her from the outside." Socrates made the same point as well.

king of the Jews?" Jesus responds, "Are you asking this from yourself, or did someone tell you about me?" In other words, *"Are you thinking for yourself, or just repeating what someone else told you?"* The real lesson we are supposed to take from the great spiritual Teachers of humanity, is not that we should grovel in blind faith, but that we must learn how to think from our own authentic self. Jesus even tells his followers, in simple and clear language (that we routinely ignore), that the truth cannot be found outside us, we must turn our trust *inward:*

> *Once Jesus was asked by the Pharisees when the*
> *kingdom of God was coming, and he answered,*
> *"The kingdom of God is not coming with things*
> *that can be observed; nor will they say,*
> *'Look, here it is!' or 'There it is!'*
> *For, in fact, the kingdom of God is within you."*
> *(Luke.17.20-21)*

More than a thousand years earlier, Moses taught his followers exactly the same lesson:

> *Surely, this instruction which I enjoin upon you this*
> *day is not too baffling for you, nor is it beyond*
> *reach. It is not in the heavens, that you should say,*
> *"Who among us can go up to the heavens and get it*
> *for us and impart it to us, that we may observe it?"*
> *Neither is it beyond the sea, that you should say,*
> *"Who among us can cross to the other side of the*
> *sea and get it for us and impart it to us, that we*
> *may observe it?" No, the thing is very close to you,*
> *in your mouth and in your heart, to observe it.*
> *(Deut.30.11-14)*

If we do awaken *Nous* and apprehend reality, our soul "perceives the self-existence of Truth and Right, and calms itself with knowing that all things go well." But most of the time we are so enthralled with all the goings-on in the outer material world that we fail to listen to that 'still small voice' within. And yet, we can never hear these things in anyone's voice but our own, it will not be in words that others have spoken or in experiences that others have had. "I'm concerned that people should trust and look into their own soul," agreed Anthony Damiani, "and never mind expecting to find a solution by looking up theories, history, facts, things like that."[25] If we hear this voice at all, it will emerge completely fresh and new from within ourselves, in this 'here and now' moment.

We can loosely say that the past existed: but no more. We can loosely say that the future *will* exist: but not yet. It is only *now* that matters, for that is all we ever actually experience. But even 'now' does not truly exist in a concrete objective sense: it is nothing more than an imaginary moving juncture where the future flows into the past.

> This one fact the world hates, that the soul *becomes*; for that forever degrades the past, turns all riches to poverty, all reputation to a sham, confounds the saint with the rogue, shoves Jesus and Judas equally aside.... This is the ultimate fact which we so quickly reach on this, as on every topic, the resolution of all into the ever-blessed ONE.

When the world wags its finger and tells us to conform and be consistent, when it tells us to meekly head for the stable and believe what we are told, "let us enter into the state of war," cries Emerson, "and wake Thor and Woden, courage and constancy.... This is to be done in our smooth times by speaking the truth.... [H]enceforward I obey no law less than the eternal law.... I must be myself.... I do this not selfishly, but humbly and truly. It is alike your interest, and mine, and all men's, however long we have dwelt in lies, to live in truth."*

The world we live in cares less and less about that truth, less and less about the beauty, nobility and freedom of the individual. Rather, it makes every effort to mold us into obedient servants of other people's interests: we are encouraged to exchange our status as sacred, magnificent Beings for a placid life of material comfort. But real freedom is not mere comfort, nor is it about being legally allowed to do whatever silly thing we 'feel' like doing, it can never be found in a small and timid life, and it has nothing at all to do with anything that is 'out there'. Real freedom, real opportunity, real life, as Emerson taught America, can only be found in an inner mental landscape that is free from mediocrity, ignorance and conformity.

---

* Does this mean 'political correctness' is a bad thing because it puts a chill on honest speech? In some cases, absolutely. But these days we also see a counter-tendency to pounce on any sign of decency and compassion and mock it as "political correctness" and this, in my opinion, is far worse. Calling a sports team "Redskins" may seem innocuous to many people, while some Native Americans may find it degrading and offensive. Is there some 'Truth' here that we need to defend? I think not. This is certainly not what Emerson is talking about. It is one thing to suggest that people should not be overly touchy and easily offended, it is another thing altogether to boorishly insist that other people's sensitivities should be ignored or mocked when they do not coincide with mine. Political correctness can certainly get out of hand, and it should not be used to prevent people from expressing their deepest truths. But ignorance and bigotry do not pass muster as "deepest truths" in my opinion, and the suggestion that we need to override all political correctness so that every bigot can freely mouth off about his or her hatred and prejudice is far more damaging to America than "too much political correctness.".

CHAPTER FOUR

SCIENCE AND REASON

We are the heirs of 'Logical Positivism', a philosophical endeavor that seeks to impose scientific thinking into every aspect of our lives by suggesting that all forms of human knowledge should aspire to the same sort of rigorous rationality as science. According to the canons of logical positivism a statement is meaningful only if it can be determined, through sensory observations or scientific experimentation, to be either true or false: anything that cannot be analyzed in this simple manner is considered meaningless, unworthy of the concern of serious people.

Thus do we attempt to reject all the wonder and mystery of life, which means, on the one hand, that we are lying to ourselves (under the guise of being rational and intellectually sophisticated), and on the other hand, that our constricted minds have seceded from our emotions and intuitions, shattering the soul into fragments.

This viewpoint separates the visible world of matter (which we can supposedly analyze objectively and which therefore is considered exclusively 'real'), from the invisible world of mind (which cannot be analyzed objectively and must therefore be considered 'not real'). The 'real world' portrayed by this positivist science has quantities but no qualities, and is without significance. *Quantities* are objective characteristics which can be measured, weighed, or counted. These are not matters of opinion. But *qualities* can be debated. Subjective qualities impart meaning, color and significance to our experience, but meaning disintegrates in a world where everything, even our thoughts, emotions, aspirations, etc. are believed to be nothing more than measurable quantities.

As we have already noted, none of us live in such a world, dense with numerical calculations but devoid of meaning.[26] Our arms do not rise up due to mere laws of mechanics: we raise them deliberately because we desire to take hold of something. Even a lost dog seeking its home is not moving its four limbs aimlessly. A sharp division between consciousness and the physical world is annulled by these fundamental observations, and a rigid obsession with such distinctions only serves to distort the truth of our actual *experience*.

Nonetheless, science can find no purpose intrinsic to nature. It only finds linear formulas of succession[27]: this event causes the next event. By themselves, none of these formulas offer any reason for their own existence. *Why* should material objects attract each other with a force of gravity proportional to their mass? *Why* should light travel at a speed of 186,000 miles per second and not some other speed? There is nothing inherently necessary or rational about these natural laws. "Of course", notes Alfred North Whitehead, "it is always possible to work oneself into a state of complete contentment with an ultimate irrationality. The popular positivistic philosophy adopts this attitude."[28] If these mechanical laws and formulas of succession do exist for a reason, if they do testify to any sort of importance or meaning, this cannot be disclosed by a science which simply gathers the data.

When knowledge is reduced to mere objective data, devoid of understanding and wisdom, it leads to what Douglas Sloan has called "our exquisitely stupid cleverness".[29] Our knowledge may certainly lead to exquisitely clever technology, but rarely is it put to the service of human dignity or conscience, since, under the influence of logical positivism, we presume that statements of 'conscience' do not carry the same weight as statements of 'scientific fact'. This leaves us with very little motivation for considering the consequences of our actions on humanity, life, or creation in general. The scientific imperative, 'if it *can* be done it *must* be done', replaces any moral imperative, as well as most common sense. Our cleverness remains exquisite, but put to the service of vulgar consumerism and endless war, it all too often indeed becomes 'stupid'.

~

For several hundred years, the scientific examination of the world has been dependent on two primary assumptions:

- Individual bits of matter can be isolated and studied objectively, unaffected by other matter and unaffected by the person making the examination.

- In making observations, our senses provide us with accurate, trustworthy information.

Both of these assumptions have been proven false. Oddly enough, modern physics (the parent science) and logical positivism are now found to be incompatible.

First of all, the assumption that one single detail can be studied in pure objective isolation is a fiction. Bits of matter cannot be extracted from time and space. There is always a *context*, there is always an environment which ceaselessly flows and changes. Every supposed 'objective fact' which scientific experimenters attempt to study in a quiet laboratory, is rushing through time from its past actualities to its future potentialities, is vibrating wildly and exchanging energies with all the atomic particles in its environment, and is being affected by whatever experimental devices the scientist is employing for purposes of study. In fact, every act of observation is itself an intervention: merely shining a light on the object we are looking at bombards it with countless photons; a small movement of our eyes is enough to set off a chain reaction affecting countless nearby atomic particles in the air.

In other words, every act of *studying* the world *alters* the world. For this reason, scientific experimenters take steps to isolate a bit of matter *as much as possible*: that is, they remove as many variables as possible from the experimental environment. But in doing so, the material they are examining is artificially withdrawn from its real nature. For instance, when researchers consider the effects of a chemical that is found polluting a stream, they attempt to measure only *its* effect on human health. But no such chemical can ever affect human health except in combination with other chemicals and the whole myriad of physical, psychological, and environmental factors that are all simultaneously affecting health, including all of history and the ongoing passage of time. Such isolation is therefore only partially possible, never completely possible. This is not because of technical difficulties that may one day be overcome. This is because of the nature of the world we live in, a world of endless movement, process, and inter-connectivity.*

Secondly, there is no such thing as a pure perception, passing directly from the external world of visible matter into the internal world of conscious awareness, unchanged and unaffected, and yielding pure, accurate and complete information. On the contrary, all of our perceptions are colored by the state of our sense organs, our memories and beliefs, and our various attitudes and feelings.

Initially, the sense organs themselves determine what can *be* perceived. Amongst the infinite number of electro-magnetic wavelengths, for instance, only a very few find receptor cells inside the retina of a healthy human eye: other creatures have receptor cells for other wavelengths, and infinite alternatives are theoretically possible. The point is that only a very limited number of vibrations cause a reaction inside the human ear: higher and lower vibrations can cause reactions in the ears of other creatures. Even within the human species there are many variations: for instance, some people can taste certain substances which others cannot. All

---

* A wonderful example of the remarkable interrelatedness and unity of all life on Earth can be seen in a four-minute video "How Wolves Change Rivers" by George Monbiot.
https://www.youtube.com/watch?t=65&v=ysa5OBhXz-Q

told, we may 'see' less than 1% of the electromagnetic spectrum and hear less than 1% of the acoustic spectrum. This means that the information about the world which our five senses provide for us is an *extremely small and specialized part* of a very big picture. If Nature had seen fit to develop our retinas with receptor cells that responded to other electromagnetic wavelengths, we would 'see' a different version of the world, just as certain animals apparently see a different version of the world. The particular limitations of our senses can hardly be said to determine what the world 'really' looks like. *They only determine which few components of this immense reality happen to be apprehensible to us*. "It is entirely possible," noted Albert Einstein, "that behind the perception of our senses, worlds are hidden of which we are unaware."

In addition to realizing that the make-up of our sense organs determines the amount of information that can potentially be received, we have also learned that before we can see something it has to be *something we already believe can plausibly exist*. In other words, nineteenth century scientists assumed that our mental functions are not part of the world we are observing, and that whatever we look at we will see. But this is clearly *not the case*. There is a famous report that when one of Captain Cook's sailing vessels was moored off the coast of a certain primitive society, the natives could not see the ship. They must have seen something, of course – perhaps a large animal or a cloud. But they had no conceptions, and no words, to describe such a thing as a gigantic floating vessel, and without this prior conception they *simply could not see it*. The ship's crew, on the other hand, saw a familiar sailing vessel – because that is what they were *able* to perceive in accordance with their prior conceptions.[30]

Einstein clearly understood this point and its significance. After entertaining the idea that scientists should

---

* Perhaps this is what William Blake was thinking about when he said, "If the doors of perception were cleansed, everything would appear to man as it truly is... Infinite."

deal only with objective measurements, he came to realize that when scientists look into the world they can only see what their prior concepts, beliefs, and thoughts, *allow* them to see – and this is precisely the opposite of the traditional scientific assumption that first we observe the world as it 'really is', and *then* we figure out our theories to explain it. When Werner Heisenberg claimed to have restricted himself to observable magnitudes (quantifiable measurements) in developing his own discoveries, Einstein said to him, "You don't seriously believe that none but observable magnitudes go into a physical theory?" But, protested Heisenberg, that is what *you* did! "Possibly I did use this kind of reasoning," Einstein continued, "but it is nonsense all the same.... [O]n principle it is quite wrong to try founding a theory on observable magnitudes alone. In reality the very opposite happens. It is the theory which decides what we can observe."[31] In other words, our prior conceptions decide what we can (or cannot) perceive.* (Einstein never conformed his thinking to anyone else, and he never worried about consistency or what other people thought. His genius was his willingness and ability to reconsider his theoretical assumptions and previous conceptions, much as Socrates taught his students to do, and to open his mind to other possibilities no matter how strange or impossible they seemed.)

So the world that we perceive is a joint function of physical features (including the object being observed and our sense organs with their limited capabilities), plus mental features (our prior ideas, beliefs and conceptions).

Now let's look at a related question: What does it mean to say "we perceive" something? What exactly *is* a 'sense perception'? In other words, how do these two dissimilar occurrences blend together:

---

* There is a corollary to this, looked at from a different angle and very much worth remembering, in Napoleon Hill's aphorism: "Whatever the mind of man can conceive and believe, it can achieve."

70

1)   An *external event in the physical world* that stimulates one or more of our senses, and,

2)   A cognitive *internal 'experience of awareness'* *of* that external event.

What I mean is this: Suppose I am standing at one end of a large field watching some children play tag at the other end of the field. Two things are occurring:

(1) there is the *external event in the physical world* – i.e., the children playing tag – which is occurring 'over there';

(2) when I *see* them playing tag, I have an *experience of awareness* of what they are doing. My *experience,* however, is *not* 'over there.' My *experience of seeing* takes place right here, where I am.

The question is, how does something that is *physically happening* 'over there' become part of my *intangible experience* 'in here'?

Perhaps the question seems trivial. We all know that through the intermediary activity of one of the five sense organs, we become aware of some aspect of the environment: we see, hear, smell, taste, or feel, some thing which is outside of our awareness itself. We see or touch a tree, for instance, and we therefore become aware of the tree.

But this seemingly obvious statement actually conceals one of those precarious occasions when we casually speak of something spectacularly ineffable as if we knew what it meant. When we say we 'become aware' of a tree, what are we talking about? What does this mean?!

To clarify the question, consider the act of vision. We can scientifically analyze this thing we call 'seeing' quite substantially as follows:

Rays of light bounce off the tree and enter the eye. The light traverses the lens, which, due to the laws of optics, flips the light ray upside down and focuses it on the back wall of the eye chamber. This inner wall is lined with tiny nerve endings called rods and cones. The rods and cones are stimulated by the energy of the light, and they respond by sending electrical transmissions down the Optic Nerve. This nerve reaches its endpoint deep within the brain in a section we call the 'visual area'. The multitude of brain cells that comprise the 'visual area' now receive the electrical stimulation transported to them by the optic nerve, and they respond with a great flurry of electrical activity of their own.

We can then analyze this activity at the profound level of the atoms and molecules that comprise these brain cells, and we discover that their constituent protons, neutrons and electrons react to the incoming electrical impulse by changing their positions and rates of vibration.

And then we see the tree.

And then we see the tree? *When? How?* When our atoms start to vibrate differently? But we do not see vibrating atoms. We see an object 'out there'. What does the *cognitive experience* of envisioning a tree have to do with vibrating atoms in the back of the skull? Where is the link between these two utterly disparate things? Our description of physiological phenomena deep within the tissues of the brain has only gotten us further *away* from the tree itself.

We have learned about many physiological and electrochemical processes that occur concurrently when we see something, but in no way does this explain what 'seeing' *is*. There remains a huge and critical *gap* between our knowledge of vibrating particles and our 'awareness' of a tree.

This inscrutable gap lies between *Matter* (which includes the tree, the sense organs, and the vibrating atoms in the *brain*), and *Consciousness* (an invisible subjective 'experience of awareness' occurring within the *mind*). Objective scientific analysis can provide no logical connection between the two: once we begin to speak of invisible subjective experience, we are completely outside its realm. Neither can Reason explain it away.

We find ourselves between worlds, *between* the Mind and the Senses, *between* the unmanifest realm of Consciousness and the manifest realm of Matter.

How does a 'sense perception' cross over into 'mind'?
How does an impression pass beyond the senses and
the vibrating atoms, traverse the mysterious 'gap', and
sink into the awareness of consciousness?

Could there be something which fills this gap, something that is unique and distinct yet partakes of both Mind and Body, something that can guide an impression through the mysterious passageway between them?

Long ago, Plato gave us a clue. In the *Symposium*, Socrates states that the 'Messenger' who transmits messages between gods and humans, i.e., between Heaven and Earth, is *Eros*. *Eros* is *desire* – not merely desire of the sexual sort, but the desire for all that is beautiful, good, and true. According to Plato's teachings, then, the messenger-between-worlds is found in the realm of human passion, feeling, and emotion.

Twenty-four hundred years later, Alfred North Whitehead[32] would recognize that within a human being the *very same thing happens* in the 'gap' we have been discussing between the external world of the body's material *senses* (analogous to 'Earth') and the internal world of the mind's invisible *consciousness* (analogous to 'Heaven'): That is, when a sense perception enters the body, resonating memories immediately arouse *feelings*. Feelings are partly of the tangible body and partly of the intangible mind.* Like

---

* Consider the emotion of fear, which contains worried and uneasy thoughts combined with sensations of a 'pit in the stomach'; or sadness, which combines thoughts of sorrow and regret with a welling up of tears and pain in the solar plexus.

Eros, these emotions can travel back and forth between the two domains of Mind and Body. These mediating feelings then transform the physical perceptions within the Brain into conscious awareness within the Mind. Precisely *how* they accomplish this transmutation may always remain a mystery.

Following this sequence in the opposite direction, Whitehead saw that when the mind conceives a thought it assigns it some gradation of *importance.* This awareness of importance arouses *interest,* which again brings in *feeling.* Once apprehended by feeling, the idea is ferried across the 'gap', from the mind to the body, where it can then be expressed outwardly. (Words being but one form of expression. Some ideas are better expressed by images, by gestures, by music, by silence.)

The point of all this is: along with the physical make-up of our sense organs, and the prior beliefs and conceptions that we carry in our minds, *the state of our emotions* is also critical to the kind of world our minds perceive (and, as we shall see in the next chapter, the kind of bodily health we experience).

In summary, we see that our ability to receive impressions from the physical world into consciousness, holistically depends on the natural history of the species, the general health and genetics of the body, the memories, beliefs and conceptions within the mind, and perhaps most importantly, the emotions of the heart. This is why the sharp division between mind and matter, between body and soul, is an illusion. It is yesterday's science. In modern science a world of flowing energies, complex relationships, and essential interdependence has taken the place of the dead, mechanical world of separate little particles banging around in empty space. The 'onlooker' stance of earlier scientific thinking, which saw man as an irrelevant spectator of this dead universe, has been completely altered by fresh understandings of flowing patterns of mutuality and wholeness, since even the simplest act of observation is itself an intervention, with repercussions throughout the natural world and reciprocal repercussions throughout the observer's mind.

Beyond Reason

We have seen that when science has learned everything it can possibly learn about eyes and neurons and electrical energy, it will still not be able to explain what seeing *is*. It may ultimately be able to give us a complete description of the biological, chemical and physical events that occur *when* we see, but the miracle itself will remain outside its understanding. This is not because there is something wrong with science, and it is not because a necessary piece of scientific knowledge has not yet been discerned (but eventually will be). It is a consequence of precisely what science is all about. Science is descriptive only. It ultimately explains nothing. It can describe *how* things happen (formulas of succession), but it is not the concern of science to ask *why*.

That is *our* job. The dignity of men and women – what makes it possible for us to be different from other creatures – lies in our individual concern with this question.

When we fail to recognize the limitations of science, we fall prone to the worship of science. To pronounce with pompous certainty that something has been 'proven scientifically' and must therefore be accepted as the last word on the subject, is inconsistent with the meaning of science itself as well as with human reason. There are two excesses that must be avoided: to exclude rational scientific thinking, and to admit nothing but rational scientific thinking. Science becomes 'scientism' when the pursuit of scientific objectivity becomes a fetish, notes Stephen Larsen. Scientism is an absolutist and fundamentalist way of thinking that insists on believing in "a hybrid view of reality cobbled together from Newtonian physics and tenth-grade science."[33]

75

As science and philosophy continue to examine and unravel the mysteries of the relationship between the inner experiences of mind and the external events of matter, we stand in an ideal position to begin a fresh examination of the universe. But Reason finds itself stymied by the stubborn refusal of 'actual reality' to reveal itself. As Plato knew, if one wishes to know actual reality, reason (and in particular, our fetish with *only* examining the world through the filter of so-called 'scientific objectivity') *has to give way*. This has always been the stance of mystics: "Evolution is not finished," wrote the Indian philosopher and mystic, Sri Aurobindo, and "reason is not the last word nor the reasoning animal the supreme figure of Nature."[34] But it has also had adherents in western science: "Reason's last step", as famously noted by Blaise Pascal, "is the recognition that there are an infinite number of things which are beyond it. It is merely feeble if it does not go as far as to realize that."[35] This overused quote is often misunderstood. The kind of realization that Pascal is referring to here is not 'irrational' or 'anti-rational', nor is it 'anti-science'. There is no question that many critics of science *do* argue from the tiresome and fatuous standpoint of irrationality, but Pascal is talking about something else, something that the West seems to keep forgetting: he is referring to the possibility of reaching a *higher* form of knowing. He is talking about *Nous*.

Socrates knew that *Eros* is required to lure Reason to its final extremity, where it recognizes its own limitations. Along the way, at its most productive, Reason accompanied by *Eros* is grounded in feelings of interest in the subject, feelings of devotion to truth, enjoyment in discovery, and an appreciation for beauty and mystery. But Reason without *Eros*, dried up of feeling and separated from any worthy aim, becomes preoccupied with pointless scurrying about, busily ripping apart the tapestry of life, analyzing all the pieces, classifying them, but unable to remember why or how to put them back together again.

I do not think it is an exaggeration to say that all truly ground-breaking knowledge comes from noetic insight *beyond* reason. Old thought patterns dissolve and something new appears. Discursive reasoning, logic, experimentation and classification, can all help to prepare the ground for the soul to awaken and for insight to occur, but they do this by simply rearranging what is already known. Only erotic longing, in the fullest sense (that inner sacred *desire* for all that is beautiful, good, and true), can lead us beyond such circular processes and open up new possibilities of awareness. When we cherish this longing, remembering what it is and what it means for our lives, we see that *Eros* is the link between meaningless data and meaningful wisdom. All those subjects that teach the soul about meaning – philosophy, art, music, literature, theology, poetry – are then enlivened and refreshed once again, for they provide the soul with a depth of understanding that is essential for the mature pursuit of science, that carries far more 'weight' than mere technological knowledge. And then this technological knowledge gains a context of meaning and purpose that allows it to become, appropriately, the highly regarded servant, but not the master, of humanity.

~

Emerson, Plato, the Bible, etc., present the visible world as grounded in a higher order of reality, which is the source of life and life's meaning, and which is only accessible through higher levels of Mind. This, of course, is a complete inversion of the dominant scientific view. In the scientific scheme of things, life and consciousness are merely by-products of the accidental motions of inanimate matter. According to the much older tradition, however, life and consciousness are the *primary* characteristics of reality: matter is the secondary offspring.

It is not self-evident that only one or the other of these viewpoints is singularly true.

In its recognition of higher and lower levels of reality, the tradition places the human being in a unique position within the hierarchy, i.e., squarely in the middle as a 'Microcosm', a tiny recapitulation of the full essential nature of the universe. On the one hand, human beings possess all the essential characteristics of minerals, plants, and animals. And yet, at the same time, unlike these lower forms, we can also be open to levels of reality that transcend the visible world.

A human being, standing at the *midpoint* of the creative order, is thus potentially capable of intuiting meaning, truth, goodness, and divinity. This is the quintessential human quality. *This is what makes a human being human.* And as a consequence of being intimate with both nature and divinity, the tradition imposes responsibilities upon human beings: we are "our brother's keeper", we are "the stewards of the earth."[36]

When engaged in our scientific way of knowing, on the other hand, a human being stands in requisite isolation *outside* of the creation, as an inquiring, analytic, 'onlooker'. But as a spectator to life and creation, science itself has no, and needs no, intrinsic system of ethics: ethics must come from *within life*. Unfortunately, Douglas Sloan notes, because this detached modern endeavor is so little informed by traditional wisdom, "With all our mushrooming know-how and frenzied hurry to transform the world out of all recognition, if not indeed out of existence, we are increasingly helpless and confused in the face of the world we are creating."[37] A moment's reflection upon the stunning developments taking place each day in the worlds of computers, weaponry, genes, and clones, provides sufficient verification for this statement.

Socrates declared that the soul is immortal. This may or may not be true. But the truth of this statement cannot be decided one way or another by anything scientists have to tell us. In fact, as we have said, a purely quantitative science contributes nothing to the great questions of human existence. Explications of the 'lower' do not explain all the complexity and miraculousness of the 'higher'. A reductive analysis of the 'parts' will never grasp the meaning of the 'whole'. Quantitative measurements cannot explain our essential human qualities.

Science and its companion, realism, cannot be dismissed: but they can and must be questioned. If the great questions and issues still move us, we cannot turn to science for much help. This responsibility cannot be delegated.

Once again, we can and we must do our own thinking.

CHAPTER FIVE

ON HEALING

Just as our children's minds are not soulless mechanical devices that can be repaired or upgraded with standardized rote education, so our bodies are not merely physical machines that can be repaired or upgraded with chemicals. We are physical, emotional, psychological, social, and spiritual beings. To be truly healthy, all aspects of our being must be functioning properly in themselves, and in a balanced, appropriate, relationship with each other and with the world.

For all our impressive and sophisticated modern knowledge, it remains true that we still have much to learn about our bodies, our hearts and minds, our species, and our planet. Meanwhile, armed with an incomplete understanding of ourselves and each other, we face the most terrifying of times. We do not know whether we shall destroy ourselves first with economic collapse, environmental collapse, infectious pandemics, race violence, religious war, or a nuclear holocaust. In the face of all this pending horror, our tendency is often *not* to fight for our lives with every reasonable and heroic effort we can muster: our tendency is to numb ourselves with television, the internet, drugs, pornography, and gossip – and to ignore the reasonable and the heroic, because they seem either too boring, too naïve, or both.

Two questions are at issue in this chapter: (1) what *is* health, and (2) what is our *responsibility* to our own health, to each other's health, and to the planet's health – because if you or I were ever to become totally, optimally, and gloriously healthy, while the whole world goes to hell around us, we would have done nothing very important.

The marketplace is filled with books, seminars, and websites, telling us what healing is and how to attain it. But all this fragmented information has become unwieldy and confusing. In the face of this, I am going to suggest a simple unified theory of healing that is based on the age-old understanding of the threefold nature of the universe: in other words, I am going to suggest an inclusive, coherent, definition of 'Holism'. In addition to bringing some clarity to the discussion, I hope this will challenge much of the ingrained, orthodox, scientistic *way of thinking* about health and disease that sees illness as an invading entity that must be destroyed. When health care is concerned only with combatting disease and symptoms, it allows us to engage in the dangerous illusion that we can keep doing everything wrong – to ourselves, to each other, and to the planet – and that we will somehow "get away with it." As long as scientists find a cure for heart disease, we can keep eating badly. As long as scientists find a cure for cancer, we can keep polluting the environment. As long as scientists find cures for stress-related illnesses, we can keep living lives filled with tension, negativity, and quiet desperation. But everything in this universe must be paid for, as devotees of Karma Yoga and fiscal conservatism both well know. No one "gets away" with anything. Because we do not remember this, we have given ourselves over to a cycle of unconscious and conscience-less self-destruction and mass destruction. Cancer, stroke, diabetes, chronic inflammatory and autoimmune syndromes, among other modern scourges, are not going away. Waiting for a magical cure is a deadly mistake. Waiting for a magical invention to save us from environmental destruction or nuclear annihilation, while we continue to damage the environment, stockpile nuclear weapons, and fill the world with hatred, is the same deadly mistake on even more terrifying levels. We make this mistake on *many* levels. We look for something for nothing. We forget that we have to pay. We forget that it is up to *us*. Either we must now take responsibility for changing the situation we are in, or it is going to be 'lights out'. And the change has to begin with changing *the way we think*.

Of course, things are looking up in many ways. Today, even the most stubbornly orthodox medical practitioner will no longer deny that many, if not most, of our modern healthcare problems could be avoided, improved, and sometimes even healed, by paying better attention to diet, exercise, relaxation, and emotional happiness. Nonetheless, while we look for ways to cut medical costs and get insurance coverage for everyone without destroying the economy, it seems lost on many people that the vast majority of our healthcare problems could be dramatically improved through nothing more earth-shattering than switching to a healthy, natural diet. And this intransigence remains at work throughout society, despite the fact that eating well is not a dreary, unfair 'punishment'. Wholesome, nutritious foods are delicious and enjoyable. Eating well means living well, with love and respect for ourselves, for each other, and for the Earth.

~

The threefold idea that I mentioned above is the ancient idea that everything that comes into being has three inherent 'forces' or qualities: an active force, a receptive force, and a conciliating force. This simply means that something must 'act' (the active force), something must 'receive' (the receptive force), and something must mediate between them and determine the precise relationship that eventuates (the conciliating force).

Perhaps the simplest way of seeing this idea at work is in chemistry. In a basic chemical experiment, a chemical, called here a re-agent, is placed in a test tube (this represents the receptive force waiting to be acted upon). Another chemical is then added, to act upon the first one (this is called the agent, representing the active force). But nothing happens until a third force, a 'catalyst', is added, that arouses and guides the interaction between the agent and re-agent (the catalyst might be a third chemical, it might be heat – from placing the test tube over a Bunsen burner – or it may simply be the physical act of shaking the ingredients. In the *bio*chemical reactions that take place within our bodies, *enzymes* [often vitamins] are typically the catalysts.) This universal concept can be seen in many other places as well, from the three basic components of the atom, to the Christian Trinity, to the three branches of government.

By applying this idea to the issues of disease causation and how the body heals, a lot of troubling enigmas can be simplified: Why do some people get sick while others break all the rules and remain healthy? If tobacco is a carcinogen, why do some smokers not get cancer? Why do some people practically live on candy, saturated fat, and emotional negativity, and never get ill? Why do certain measures help one patient, yet fail with another? Why do some things come back, some never go away, and others just go away for good by themselves?

The primary answer to all these questions is that we are all different, we are not merely mechanical devices that can be 'fixed' by following some sort of standardized medical instruction manual. But more to the point, *no one thing is ever responsible for any disease*. Rather, *three* inter-reacting factors are simultaneously necessary in every case:

1) There must be an Active force – that is, something detrimental must *act* on the body. This could be a virus, a bacterium, a poison, radiation, trauma, and so forth.

    But these things are ceaselessly in contact with our bodies, yet we do not all continually fall sick *en masse*. So there has to be more to it than just this. (Needless to say, one or another of these active agents might sometimes be so overwhelming that the other forces are rendered virtually irrelevant – a massive dose of lethal radiation for instance. But this is the exception to the rule, not the general rule, and even in cases of massive poisoning or epidemic infections there is typically some small number of survivors, indicating that other factors are involved.)

84

2) There must be a Receptive force – that is, something in the body, sometimes referred to as the 'ground', must be already weakened or out-of-balance and thus receptive to being abnormally acted upon. For instance, it might be a gut lining inflamed because of poor nutrition, a liver weakened by long-term drug or alcohol abuse, a congenitally weak heart, or any tissue that has been overwhelmed by the degenerative effects of long-term stress.

But even if such an Active/Receptive combination occurs and the body takes a turn toward illness, we have massive disease-controlling abilities: the immune system, the hormonal system, the nervous system, etc., should spring into action. So if our natural healing forces do not put a stop to this, there must still be something else going on.

3) There must be a Conciliating force – something inside us, against all of nature's best intentions, must inappropriately allow, or perhaps even encourage, the sickness to take hold and persist: more precisely, it must fail to prevent the body from *stopping* the active agent that is damaging the receptive tissue. This 'something' is usually most perceptible as a malfunctioning immune system. And here is the key which we will discuss at length in a moment: the strength and viability of our immunity (and *all* our disease-fighting capabilities) is a joint function of physical, emotional, psychological, and spiritual factors.

This is why not all cigarette smokers get cancer. Tobacco *is* a carcinogen, but if a particular smoker was born with a "good constitution", if he or she eats well, exercises, and takes good care of the body in other ways, then he or she may (the operative word is 'may') luck out and not give the carcinogen enough weakened tissue to act upon. Or, if he or she has a really positive inner emotional and psychological life, then perhaps the immune system will simply not allow any cancerous activity to get out of control.

Despite these possibilities, I implore you not to risk it. Don't smoke. Life is risky enough.

Looked at from the opposite perspective, many people are warm, loving, even happy-go-lucky, and *do* get cancer. Some people jog and eat plenty of fresh vegetables and *do* get heart disease. Things are not as simple or linear as we might like them to be. It all comes down to matters of proportion and blending among three simultaneous causes, some within our control (e.g., diet, exercise, etc.), and some not in our control (e.g., genetics – though I reserve the right to partially revise this statement later on when we talk about epigenetics). So the particular pieces of the puzzle that comprise the three factors will differ in every individual case (a bacterium here, a virus there, a poor diet here, a poor attitude there), but *there will always be a triad of these three fundamental 'forces'* behind any illness.

Turning now from the cause of illness to the process of healing, the same three forces are at work.

1) An Active force for repair of damaged tissue must be activated or added to the body. In other words, the body must start doing its job again. This may happen naturally with no outside help, or it may be enhanced by outside help in the form of some kind of actively-stimulating healing remedy (a medicinal drug, an herbal remedy, etc.) or healing technique (a chiropractic or osteopathic adjustment, an acupuncture treatment, etc.), or something else that either artificially replaces a malfunctioning bodily process (typically the job of western medicine or surgery, and often necessary) or, better yet, *nudges the body itself back into appropriate action.*

2) Meanwhile, the damaged, unbalanced tissue must now become receptive to the healing process. This is

where basic good health habits come into play (nutrition, exercise, relaxation, hygiene, etc.), so that the tissues of the body no longer present an obstacle to healing but provide a healthy 'ground' where healing can easily take place. If our physical bodies are so badly cared for as to be unreceptive to healing, then no medicine, no technique, no remedy, and no amount of happiness are likely to help very much.

3) Finally, in order for the active healing forces in the body to be capable of repairing the damaged-but-now-receptive tissue, the overall psyche must be in a state in which the great tendency (consciously or not) is in the direction of life and health. The state of our psyche, through its powerful interventions in the cardiovascular, endocrine, nervous, and immune systems, provides this third healing force that either reconciles a poisonous substance and weak tissue to disease, or reconciles a healing action and strong tissue to health.

Again, even though the specific details will vary with each individual case, the overall blueprint of a Triad of Healing (this all-embracing threefold blueprint is how I define 'Holistic') is present in every case.

All three forces are critically necessary, but the third factor, in my opinion, is the most important consideration in healing, both because of its extraordinary potential power and because it is often given such short shrift in our mechanistic culture.

We have all heard the words, spoken dismissively, "Oh, that's just the placebo effect." We know that it is possible for someone to feel better, and for symptoms to go away, merely because they mistakenly believed they were given real medicine.

"Just" the placebo effect? "Merely" because they believed? Hearing these sentiments never ceases to astonish me. I would submit that the placebo effect – the ability of our consciousness to dramatically affect the physical world – is arguably the most powerful force in the universe. In fact, in this scenario it assures us that we have immense power to heal ourselves, without needing much or any help from medical doctors, chiropractors, herbalists, or anybody else. It is a force that must be harnessed, and this is certainly not easy: but if we are able to harness it, it is a force beyond anything that pharmaceutical companies could ever come up with.

Unless you left college very recently, you have been taught that the DNA in our genes determines our anatomical characteristics and our physiological processes, and their decisions are absolute and unchangeable – as a result, if we happen to be prone to certain illnesses or physical complaints, or are otherwise dissatisfied with our physical makeup, it is simply too bad: we are victims of our genes.

But it turns out we are *not* victims of our genes, except in the rarest of cases. Only about 2% of the population suffer from those devastating problems that are inexorably caused by a defective or missing gene: aside from possible symptomatic relief, it is sadly true that little can be done about this (though hopefully some wonderful future research will find a way to alter the chromosomal structure). For most of us, however, the conventional belief that our genetic makeup determines our fate, turns out to be not-so-true after all. Recent discoveries in epigenetics, a new branch of biology that studies how environmental signals are translated into gene expression, have changed all that.

The first thing to understand is that around each strand of DNA is a protein 'sleeve.' This sleeve serves as a barrier between the information contained in the DNA strand and the rest of the intracellular environment. DNA provides a blueprint for how new proteins are to be formed (most of our physical structure – our muscles, organs, etc. – as well as most of the enzymes that determine how internal chemical processes will proceed – are made of protein). In order for the blueprint in the DNA to be 'read' so that the protein can be made, the sleeve around that piece of DNA has to be unwrapped so the information is available. Otherwise, it cannot be acted upon and the blueprint in the DNA lies dormant. So what has to happen is that some kind of 'signal' must arrive at the protein sleeve to 'tell' it that a piece of the DNA it is covering is needed and it has to unravel at that spot. Once this happens, the code is recognized by other cellular elements and the particular protein molecule is assembled: this is what biologists mean when they say that a gene is "expressed".

Two important questions arise: (1) what kind of 'signals' cause the protein sleeve to unravel and allow the gene's message to be read and acted upon ("expressed"), and (2) is that gene's information "written in stone" as we say, so that nothing can ever be done to alter it and we are at its mercy?

Let's assume for the moment that all 'signals' are in fact chemicals. The proteins comprising the 'sleeve' have receptors that recognize particular chemicals as signals that, when touched, spur them into action. It is easy enough to imagine that if a particular protein is lacking somewhere, this could cause a chemical response, and the chemical that is released will cross the cell membrane and slide over to the protein sleeve surrounding the DNA and cause it to open up.

But this simple statement actually reveals something extremely important. The point is that our genetic activity is *not determined by the genes themselves.* On the contrary, our genetic activity is determined by *influences in the cell's environment* that cross the membrane into the cell. In other words, it is the *environment* that causes our 'fate', not our DNA. And yes, we can affect our cells' environment in many, many ways. This is why I reserved the right to alter my previous statement that our genes are beyond our control. We are *not* 'helpless victims' of our genes.

For instance, suppose you have a gene that, if expressed, increases the possibility you will develop diabetes. If the protein sleeve around that gene is never unwrapped, the gene can cause no problems. Epigenetic researchers have found that the protein sleeve can be affected by a good diet and an active lifestyle: these behaviors cause *different chemical signals* to enter the cell than if you ate poorly and had a generally unhealthy lifestyle. Furthermore, as a result of these different signals, the sleeve becomes much more difficult to unravel.

Not only does this protect *you* from diabetes despite having this gene, but the *tighter protein sleeve gets passed down through heredity* as well as the underlying gene. In other words, our lifestyle choices not only affect ourselves, but they can affect future generations as well.

~

But what about our thoughts, emotions and beliefs. Do these affect our cells' activity? Consider this: In the center of our brain is an area called the hypothalamus. Researchers have long known that the various sections of the hypothalamus are concerned with such things as pleasure, pain, sexuality, hunger, and all our emotions. Just above the hypothalamus are the two enormous cerebral hemispheres, the seat of our higher thinking functions. Thousands of nerves connect the hypothalamus with the cerebral hemispheres, which means that information about our thoughts and emotions are continually being exchanged.

The hypothalamus (and the thalamus, which controls sensory input and motor output) border an open chamber called the third ventricle, which is filled with cerebrospinal fluid. Also bordering the third ventricle are the pineal gland and the pituitary gland. The pineal gland (which some esoteric traditions believe is a physical manifestation of a 'third eye' – the 'eye of the soul') releases melatonin, which regulates sleep and may affect the immune system and have anti-aging effects, into the cerebrospinal fluid. The pineal is also probably the source for another chemical, DMT (Dimethyltryptamine), that is also found in the cerebrospinal fluid. DMT is also widespread in the plant kingdom, in plants that are commonly used in shamanic rituals. It can produce powerful near-death and mystical experiences, and is hypothesized to be released at birth, death, and during vivid dreams. It has been called "the spirit molecule".

90

The pituitary gland is called 'the master gland' because it tells the other glands of the hormonal system what to do: by sending out its own chemical signals into the bloodstream, it tells the thyroid gland when to speed up the body's metabolism by producing more thyroid hormone, it tells the adrenals when to cut down the production of cortisone, etc. Of course, it makes these decisions after receiving chemical signals *from* the other glands as well as messages from the hypothalamus. The pituitary is thus like a master conductor, listening to all the instruments and conducting the body's great chemical symphony.

But the hypothalamus *composed* the symphony, and is constantly at work changing and re-writing parts of it and sending new instructions to the conductor. It is inspired to create these new compositions in response to neural communication between higher thinking centers and its own emotional content, as well as the spiritual messages it receives from the pineal gland through chemical messages in the cerebrospinal fluid, and with continual feedback from the pituitary gland which is in constant contact with the endocrine glands throughout the body (which, again according to some spiritual traditions, are the physical representatives of the chakras, which links them to the movement of *ch'i* and the possible arousal of kundalini).

In other words, this constant communication amongst physical, emotional, intellectual and spiritual aspects of our being, causes chemical changes within the cerebrospinal fluid (which bathes the entire brain and central nervous system, exchanging information at all times), as well as all the powerful yet delicate hormones that are released by the endocrine glands (which enter the bloodstream and affect every single cell in the body in some ways that we understand, but undoubtedly also in myriad ways we have yet to discover.[*])

---

[*] The reason medical drugs have side effects is that, like hormones, once they enter the bloodstream they get into every cell in the body, not just the ones where the problem is. So the chemical not only has the desired effect, but can have *all sorts of unexpected effects all over the place.*

So here we have some of the extraordinary links between mind, heart, body, and spirit. These connections have been known for some time, assuring us that there are physical results of our thoughts, emotions and beliefs, and these physical results change the very content of our blood, they bathe and communicate with the brain, and they enter and affect every one of the trillions of cells in our bodies. Add to this the new research about DNA and how by changing the cell's environment we change our genetic expression, and we see a hint, at the very least, of the immense potential to heal ourselves that always lies within us.

~

But this entire explanation has been based on an outmoded reliance on the Newtonian view of the world as a gigantic mechanism. In the Quantum view of the world, it turns out that all of this matter we have been talking about – cell membranes, enzymes, hormones, and so forth – in fact, the whole universe – is really just energy, vibration, and potentialities that may or may not even exist. I very much enjoy the way the biologist, Bruce Lipton, describes his loss of certitude about biology when he was first confronted with the inescapable new understandings of the 'parent' science, physics:

> In retrospect, it should have been obvious to me and to other biologists that Newtonian physics, as elegant and reassuring as it is to hyper-rational scientists, cannot offer the whole truth about the human body, let alone the universe. Medical science keeps advancing, but living organisms stubbornly refuse to be quantified. Discovery after discovery about the mechanics of chemical signals, including hormones, cytokines (hormones that control the immune system), growth factors and tumor suppressors cannot

explain paranormal phenomena. Spontaneous healings, psychic phenomena, amazing feats of strength and endurance, the ability to walk across hot coals without getting burned, acupuncture's ability to diminish pain by moving "chi" around the body, and many other paranormal phenomena defy Newtonian biology.[38]

The whole concept of matter, it turns out, is a sensory illusion. Quantum physicists know that what we thought were tangible material atoms are actually swirling vortices of intangible energy that are constantly vibrating, spinning, and radiating energy. Large conglomerations of these spinning vortices – such as those that make up our cells, our organs, and all the way up to enormous conglomerations like you and me – also radiate unique vibrational signatures. But most conventional biologists and medical scientists continue to stand by the reductionist Newtonian model of reality (aside from a few unavoidable technological advances like CAT scans, MRI's, and dissolving kidney stones with harmonic frequencies) which means they willfully ignore the role that energy vibrations play in health and disease and the vast possibilities that this opens up for deepening our understanding, and for promising new avenues of treatment: and this continues, despite the fact that, using the old model, some studies show that as many as 300,000 people die each year from the adverse effects of prescribed medications. Fortunately, as time goes on, this attitude is slowly changing and more and more individual scientists and scientific organizations are exploring these new frontiers. Many others, however, will still have to be brought kicking and screaming into the future.

One thing we are interested in here is the comparison of *energy signals* as bearers of information across a cell membrane, compared to *chemical signals* (such as hormones, neurotransmitters, and other chemicals). Energetic vibrations are of course faster (virtually

93

instantaneous), and are more efficient. And they can certainly cross a membrane and affect the cell's contents. But can *specific, controllable* signals be transferred through our cell membranes to the protein sleeve via energetic vibrations? As of this moment, I know of no orthodox scientific research that has been able to verify and measure such a phenomenon, though efforts are being made: the new field of Behavioral Epigenetics has been unraveling the mechanisms by which thoughts and emotions translate into cellular changes. Part of what will be needed for such explorations to succeed, is that pervasive negative attitudes within the scientific community – what the Nobel Prizewinning physicist Brian Josephson has called "Pathological Disbelief", and what I would call scientific fundamentalism – will have to change. In addition, the dependency on pharmaceutical companies for research money (with their narrow focus on only Newtonian solutions that can make a profit) is going to have to change as well. Finally, the total reliance on linear thinking (rather than comprehensive *holistic* thinking), and the devotion to scientific reductionism as the only way to 'seriously' study the world, will also need to change.

In the meantime, I can assure you that if you choose to experience a world full of love and kindness, your body will respond in many healthy ways. If you choose to experience a world of fear and hatred, your overall health will be compromised. This cannot be 'measured'. That does not change the fact that it is true. Anecdotal and clinical evidence abound regarding the efficacy of various "energy healing" techniques (homeopathy, reiki, and many others), and the placebo effect makes it clear that the energy of consciousness most definitely can alter our health. The fact is, harnessing the power of the mind can be more effective than the drugs we have been programmed and propagandized to believe we need. To a great extent, it is precisely this programming and propagandizing that makes the drug effective to begin with: if you absolutely believe that a drug, or any other treatment, is going to be effective, and your subconscious mind agrees, then the drug or treatment will be effective. This also works in reverse: many people have gone home and died after believing that a witch doctor's evil curse had sealed their fate, and many other people have gone home and died after believing that a medical doctor's terminal prognosis had sealed their fate.

~

We know that stress causes a specific variety of responses in the body. We know that these physiological responses are healthy and valuable in moments of danger. But under *chronic* stress, when these physiological actions continue unabated because the stressful danger never ends, the mind and body can be badly damaged. Fortunately, we do have known ways to relieve stress.

When the hypothalamus recognizes danger (it may be a saber-tooth tiger, or it may be an angry boss, a sour relationship, financial hardship, a fear of crime or terrorism, etc.), it tells the pituitary to order the adrenal glands to secrete protective stress hormones into the bloodstream. These hormones do three particular things: (1) they contract blood vessels in the gut, so that during the crisis energy is not wasted on digestion, and more blood is instead shunted into the muscles of the arms and legs which may be called upon to run or fight; (2) they suppress the immune system, and the ability to inhibit or shut down inflammatory responses, again so that energy is not wasted (we can fight off the flu virus *after* we have escaped the tiger); and (3) they contract blood vessels in the forebrain (which relates to the *conscious* mind and our ability to think things through), and shunt the blood back to the hindbrain (which relates to the *subconscious* mind that runs our reflex activity): this is no time for thinking, this is the time for acting,

But if the source of stress continues and continues, if we are besieged by unresolved problems and worries, or if we are overwhelmed by unresolved fears that continue to stress us out even if the external cause has disappeared (PTSD is an extreme example of this, but it does not have to be this extreme to be a serious problem), then notice what happens: (1) our digestive system functions poorly, which can lead to a myriad of issues involving pain, malabsorption of nutrients that our cells need to maintain health and life, bowel issues, etc. (2) lowered immunity opens us up to attacks from bacteria, viruses, and other pathogens that should have been stopped, and inflammation gets out of control (evidence is rapidly accruing in research circles that a vast number of pervasive contemporary illnesses are due to chronic, uncontrolled, inflammation: diabetes, arthritis, Alzheimer's, cardiovascular disease, just to name a few); and (3) we become less able to think clearly (and some studies suggest that the inhibition of neurons by stress hormones may become a root cause of depression).

The need to break these cycles of chronic stress is why relaxation (to calm the freneticisms of the body) and meditation (to calm the freneticisms of the mind) are such critical requirements for healing.

A body filled with tension will suffer from fatigue, stiffness and pain. It may be clumsy and unattractive. It may be cut off from sensations of pain (which provide important warnings) as well as from feelings of pleasure. Chronic tension will impede the free circulation of blood, nerve energy, and *ch'i*, causing the body to deteriorate and age more quickly, and it will have difficulty recognizing or 'hearing' important signals coming from the internal or external environment. Fortunately, there are countless excellent techniques of body awareness and 'body work' that can help teach overexcited westerners how to relax.

People who practice regular meditation routinely discover not only that their health improves, but that all aspects of their lives are affected in beneficial ways: in fact, the deepest purpose of meditation is to silence the endless blathering of the chattering "monkey mind" so that, in the stillness and silence that follows, a higher divine force can descend into our being and lift our consciousness up into higher spiritual realities. But meditation is also, to be sure, a useful tool for physical healing.

According to cardiologist Bernie Siegel:

> It tends to lower or normalize blood pressure, pulse rate, and the levels of stress hormones in the blood. It produces changes in brain-wave patterns, showing less excitability. These physical changes reflect changes in attitude, which show up on psychological tests as a reduction in the competitive type A behavior that increases the risk of heart attack. Meditation also raises the pain threshold and reduces one's biological age.... In short, it reduces wear and tear on both body and mind, helping people live better and longer."[39]

~

The ultimate conclusion to be drawn from the placebo effect is not that pain and illness are "merely" in our heads, or that we are easily fooled. The placebo effect does not belittle us. It empowers us. It tells us that we have profound possibilities, and that we can take control of our health and our lives: we need never underestimate the power of the human mind, heart and soul.

Basic techniques for harnessing this power have been a standard part of people's education in many cultures, especially in the east and in aboriginal societies. These methods are not a secret. In the west, in recent centuries, these procedures have been neglected in favor of logical processes. But it turns out that our bodies do not respond to logical words and commands. *The body responds to emotional feelings and to vivid pictorial images.* Once the body and mind are calm, it is through our feelings and imagination that we can send deliberate healing instructions into our body.

The technique of mental imagery means creating mental pictures, either of desired states of being (or states of health), or of symbols that represent these states, then concentratedly imagining them in vivid detail, and repeating this exercise internally over and over again until it creates a new 'blueprint' that every cell in the body will begin to strive toward fulfilling. Rest assured that mental imagery "is not a method of self-deception," as Carl Simonton and Stephanie Matthews-Simonton noted in *Getting Well Again*. "It is a method of self-direction."[40]

Finally, simply remembering each day to take a few moments out of our stressful lives to remember what makes us happy, who and what we love, what we deeply appreciate – and to allow ourselves to *feel* these feelings – can have profound effects on our health. "I am convinced," wrote Bernie Siegel, in his classic book *Love, Medicine and Miracles*, "that unconditional love is the most powerful stimulant of the immune system. If I told patients to raise their blood levels of immune globulins or killer T cells, no one would know how. But if I can teach them to love themselves and others fully, the same changes happen automatically. The truth is: love heals."[41]

All of this is important because our psyche – mind, heart, and spirit – is the final arbiter of health and disease. At all times, our psyche, the third healing force, is either suppressing our immune system, endocrine system, and nervous system, or bolstering them. And this tells us that not only is our overall psychology a crucial factor in physical as well as mental disease, but it also reminds us that our inner life – our emotional, intellectual, and spiritual life – is as much a part of reality (or actually *more* so) as the visible physical machine called the body. It tells us that our loves and hates, our misery and happiness, our knowledge and ignorance, our apathy and aspiration, our wisdom and foolishness – all of this matters. *We* matter.

CHAPTER SIX

MY BROTHER'S AND SISTER'S KEEPER

One of the most interesting stories in *Genesis* is about Judah. You probably remember the story of how Jacob's older sons decided to get rid of their spoiled little brother, Joseph. One day when Jacob sent the boy out to see how his big brothers were doing with their flocks, they ripped off his 'coat of many colors' and threw him in a pit, and then tried to figure out what to do with him. Some wanted to kill him, but Judah suggested instead that they sell him to a caravan that was heading to Egypt, and tell Jacob that the poor kid had been devoured by wild beasts.

Joseph of course became quite a success in Egypt. Many years later, when a famine broke out in Canaan, and Jacob sent his sons to Egypt where food could still be bought, they did not realize that the powerful Viceroy of Egypt who was in charge of distributing grain was in fact their long-lost little brother. But Joseph recognized them, and he played a little game with them to see if they had changed, to see if they felt remorse, to see if they had become better men than they were when he last saw them.

But in between these two parts of the story, the author of *Genesis* interrupts and tells us a seemingly unconnected story about Judah. Here we learn that during those interim years between the caravan and the famine, Judah had married and had three sons. When the first one died and left a childless wife, Tamar, behind, the custom of the times was that the next oldest son would take her to be *his* wife. This happened as prescribed, but then Judah's second son also died. His third son, Shelah, would now be expected to marry Tamar. But Shelah was still a boy, so Judah told Tamar to return temporarily to her own father as a widow, and when Shelah was grown up they would be married.

Shelah grew to manhood, but Judah did not contact Tamar.

A long time afterward, Judah's wife passed away. After the period of mourning, he took a trip to the city of Timnah, and Tamar heard that he was going there. She also knew that Judah had not done as he should have and as he had promised, for Shelah was by now a fully grown man. Since she considered it her sacred duty to bear children, and she was considered to be betrothed to the family of Judah and could not marry anyone else, she devised a shrewd plan:

She took off her widow's garb, covered her face, and sat beside the road that led to Timnah. When Judah saw her, he did not recognize her and thought that she was a harlot, and he asked to sleep with her (the Bible is not a book for sanctimonious prudes). She asked what he would pay. He offered a young sheep from his flock. She agreed, but since he did not have the sheep with him, and was only promising to send it later, she asked for some collateral. Judah gave her his seal, cord and staff. They then slept together and she conceived (twin sons, one of whom would be the ancestor of David and Jesus). He later sent a friend to give her the sheep and retrieve his belongings, but she was nowhere to be found and no one in the region had seen any harlots.

Some months later, Judah received word that Tamar was pregnant. Since she was betrothed to his family, and Shelah had not married her, Tamar was evidently guilty of adultery – a capital offense. So Judah ordered that she be brought out and executed. As she was being brought out, she sent a package and a message to her father-in-law: "I am with child by the man to whom these belong. Examine these: whose seal and cord and staff are these?" Judah recognized them, and sparing her he said, "She is more righteous than I, inasmuch as I did not give her to my son Shelah."

When the brothers threw Joseph in the pit, they had shown no mercy. When they returned to Jacob and deceived him with Joseph's blood-splattered coat, they took no responsibility. But here, Judah admits "She is more righteous than I." This public confession of wrongdoing is the first such confession in the Bible (long overdue since Adam first blamed Eve and Eve blamed the Serpent), and it is a symbol of profound repentance. Judah has learned to be honest, to acknowledge responsibility, and to be merciful.

Years later, the trick Joseph played on his brothers was this: when they were preparing to return home with the food they had bought from him in Egypt, he instructed his deputy to secretly "Put my silver goblet in the bag of the youngest one." In the morning the brothers set off, but not far from the gates of the city they were overtaken by Joseph's deputy who accused them of stealing the goblet. The brothers, of course, were astonished, and claimed to know nothing about it. They told him go ahead and search, and they declared that if any of them were found with the cup, that brother would die and the rest would return to Joseph as his slaves. But the deputy replied that only the person who took the cup would become a slave, and the rest would go free. He then searched their belongings, from the oldest to the youngest, and the goblet turned up in young Benjamin's bag.* Horrified and heartbroken, they repacked their belongings and returned to the city.

They were brought before Joseph, who demanded to know why they had done this. Judah stepped forward and replied that God had somehow uncovered an old crime in which all the brothers were guilty, and now at last they were all prepared to pay. "Here we are, then, slaves of my lord, the rest of us as much as he in whose possession the goblet was found." But Joseph said, "Far be it from me to act thus!" Only Benjamin, he insisted, would become a slave. "The rest of you go back in peace to your father."

This is the final test. Joseph had to see if the brothers would send the youngest, Benjamin, the remaining child of Rachel, into slavery, and save their own skins. They could go free, and return home to Jacob with new lies about how his beloved Benjamin met his demise. Have they changed?

---

* Benjamin was a son of Rachel, as was Joseph. All the other brothers were the sons of Leah or Jacob's concubines.

Judah went up to him and said, "Please, my lord, let your servant appeal to my lord." He did not grovel. He went right up to him. This is the same Judah whose idea it was to sell Joseph into slavery in the first place. But *thanks to Tamar*, it is a Judah who has changed and matured. Joseph is going to be looking to see for himself whether Judah has become a *Tzadik* – a righteous man.

Judah then told him how difficult it had been for their father to let his youngest son, Benjamin, go with them on this long journey – and if he did not return, the old man would surely die of a broken heart. But Judah had promised his father that he would protect the boy. "Therefore, please, let your servant remain as a slave to my lord instead of the boy, and let the boy go back with his brothers."

Judah has passed the test. In this magnificent moment, he takes full responsibility. He shows his love for his father and his young brother. He knows what it feels like to lose two sons, and he demonstrates compassion and empathy. Long after the question was first raised by Cain, Judah finally answers it: *Yes, I am indeed my brother's (and my sister's) keeper*. Judah exemplifies the highest form of human love, without which life on earth can never succeed – the willingness to sacrifice one's life for another, which first-responders, many soldiers, and countless parents and other decent people, have demonstrated throughout the ages.

Tamar, by the way, is greatly honored in biblical tradition: she is an ancestor of both David and Christ. Like all the stories of women in the Bible, her influence is immensely significant but rarely given its due. The Bible, for obvious reasons, has a reputation and a history of sexism. But if the stories are read metaphorically and symbolically, rather than literally, they actually make very clear that spiritual development is impossible without the Sacred Feminine, and humanity is doomed if we continue to misconstrue everything that is said about the perfect equality, the required harmony, and the absolute inter-dependence of men and women.*

Women and girls have been discriminated against for far too long due to distorted fundamentalist interpretations of religion. This discrimination, attributed to a bizarre misogynistic male 'god' or some hideously twisted 'tradition', has deprived women across the world of equal rights and equal enjoyment of life for centuries. At its most repugnant, it has fostered the moronic belief that women are naturally subservient to men, and must therefore silently accept violence, rape, forced prostitution, genital mutilation, and laws that tell them what they can or cannot do with their own bodies while denying them fair access to education, healthcare, employment, and political power. As Jimmy Carter has rightly acknowledged, "The truth is that male religious leaders have had - and still have - an option to interpret holy teachings either to exalt or subjugate women. They have, for their own selfish ends, overwhelmingly chosen the latter. Their continuing choice provides the foundation or justification for much of the pervasive persecution and abuse of women throughout the world. This is in clear violation not just of the Universal Declaration of Human Rights but also the teachings of Jesus Christ, the Apostle Paul, Moses and the prophets, Mohammad, and founders of other great religions - all of whom have called for proper and equitable treatment of all the children of God. It is time we had the courage to challenge these views."[42]

~

At times, the lesson that Tamar taught Judah seems all but forgotten. Life can be so painful and difficult, all on its own – but we manage to find all sorts of reasons to hurt each other. Life can be so lonely – but we feel compelled to judge, condemn and hate each other. Life is so short – and yet, we seem obsessed with killing each other.

---

* Interested readers may wish to read further stories and interpretations of the fascinating women in the Bible in my book *The Sacred Chalice.*

Day after day, century after century, our crimes continue – crimes against ourselves, against each other, against the earth. But engrossed as we are in the frantic requirements of modern life, we cannot bear to dwell on this; and so, the art of forgetting has become an essential part of our lives. By forgetting, we become comfortable with our lives and situations. We forget any personal emptiness, we forget the sufferings of others, we forget our unmet responsibilities. This insidious comfort does indeed bring with it a certain kind of happiness. But such happiness, in the midst of pain, cynicism and meaninglessness, is surely nauseating. And none of the accoutrements of this happiness (money, sexual adventure, social status, and the like) ever quite work, because no matter how physically or emotionally comfortable they make us feel, they can never quite alleviate the discomfiting suspicion of inner nullity, or the conscience-pricking fear that there was something we forgot to do.

Notwithstanding our attempts to forget, we all know that apathy, greed, bigotry and hatred are spoiling our experience of life on earth and even threatening our very existence. What keeps us from changing this? It is as if, deep within us, we carry an odious hidden secret, hidden even from our own selves: the secret that we are not merely *willing* to give it all up, but are in fact *rushing* toward our own final destruction. Something inside us, we can only surmise, wants to die – for death will relieve our blandness and boredom, it will end the emotional pain and loneliness, and it will end our burdensome responsibilities. (But this is not really a 'secret' at all. Many centuries ago, both Virgil, in the *Aeneid*, and then Dante, in *The Divine Comedy*, described the souls waiting on the shores of the deathly River Styx as frantically pushing and shoving, desperate and eager to be the first on Charon's boat, the first to be taken away – thus depicting the great horror of our existence: the overwhelming unconscious desire to be asleep, to be dead.)

But being alive means *taking* responsibility: for ourselves, for one another, for the world, for the future. The passion to do that, however, is harder and harder to find. The longing for death, the devil within, is winning. And it is winning with incomparable ease.

This, of course, is not an exhaustive critique of human life, though it is an important one. It would certainly be pointless to dwell self-indulgently on negativity – a positive attitude can take us much further toward solutions. *But only if we are aware and informed.* We cannot allow a morbid negativity to masquerade as the whole truth, but neither can we blindly or blithely obscure harsh realities. What is needed is a deliberate psychological turning from comfortable forgetting to responsible remembering: a genuine experience of remorse for not being what we ought to be, combined with self-forgiveness, optimism, love, and a steadfast willingness to seek a better day.

We will always find the reflection of our inner lives in the external conditions of the world. In fact, we cannot change the outer world *unless* we change what we are inside – and we cannot change what we are inside until we *know* what we are inside. But because the outer world is to a great extent our own reflection, we can learn much about what we *are* (and thus follow Socrates' injunction to "Know thyself"), and what we have to *do*, by looking as objectively and clearly as we can at the world we have created.

Here in America, it will be worth our while to look at the crimes of America that exist side-by-side with our achievements, to acknowledge them and understand them and try to experience authentic remorse*, and then to consider wisely and humbly what we can do to heal the wounds these crimes have caused. From there, we can look forward with fresh optimism toward a noble and worthy future for America and the world.

---

* This is not about personal 'blame'. You and I were not there. But to simply dismiss the significance of this issue on that basis is disingenuous and solipsistic. Personal guilt is far too petty, phony, and irrelevant a response – what we are talking about is being conscious and responsible for *our national identity and our common humanity.*

The Crimes of America

There is nothing new in the observation that the two great crimes (though not the *only* crimes) of this nation have been the brutal destruction of its native people and the brutal enslavement of the black race. These two massive crimes stand in front of us always, crying out to our conscience, demanding that we never forget. Like all nations and all people, we embody both good and bad. We need to remember the bad without self-hatred, just as we need to remember the good without self-aggrandizement.

In Catholicism, the act of 'confession' has three parts. The first is the admission itself, the straightforward objective statement of acknowledgement and self-awareness. The second part is contrition: truly experiencing remorse, in our hearts and in our guts. The third part is reparation, paying for the harm we have caused. The first part is fairly easy, at least in these times when we are plainly aware of the wrongs that have been done to these two groups of people. Even the third part is relatively easy, at least in principle: economic programs and civil rights laws have gone a long way (while clearly not far enough) toward paying for what was done and ensuring it is never repeated. This is where we like to focus our energies, congratulating ourselves on how far we have come, or rebuking ourselves for not going far enough.

The second step, however, is the most difficult and perhaps the most important. Can we go further than merely creating social programs in the external world that we hope will absolve us of responsibility and allow us some peace of mind so that we can forget about it? Can we look deeply within ourselves, *beyond* mere sad feelings of guilt or sentimental pity, and confront our actual inner characteristics and motivations? Can we experience *authentic* remorse – not just for what some of our ancestors *did*, but even more importantly, for the wide disparity between what we realize *we are* (not all that different from our ancestors) and what we know we ought to *be*? Because only then could there be real amends, or real change.

In the blink of an eye, an entire people were slaughtered and an entire civilization destroyed, first by plague, then by American guns, soldiers, and unspeakable treachery. Not everything the Native American people did was noble or wonderful. They had their share of flaws, their share of violence, their share of cruelty. They also had their share of goodness, their share of wisdom, and an advanced and magnificent way of life that was very different from the Europeans who suddenly fell upon them. They had a participatory consciousness of the sacredness of life and a deep intuitive connection with the earth which was by no stretch of the imagination inferior to the state of consciousness of the violent foreign invaders who perceived them as savages, or as mere children who didn't fully appreciate 'the importance of property rights and commerce'*. These foreign invaders actually understood nothing of their reality and could not even conceive of what they were destroying: for they were not just destroying people with as much intelligence, as much love and compassion, and as much humanity as themselves, but a civilization with as much wisdom and significance as their

---

* I have heard it suggested that since Native Americans were not 'progressing' and making good 'use' of the resources of their habitat, they somehow 'deserved' to be replaced by the far more clever and progress-oriented Europeans: a phenomenally obscene and degenerate excuse for theft, murder and genocide. Actually, as noted by historian and Fulbright Scholar Al Carroll, "Spaniards were stunned by the Aztec capital being larger and more advanced than anything in Europe. Many Native cultures were more advanced than Europeans in everything but weapons. It suited the claims of conquerors to disparage Natives as primitive. One might turn this question on its head: Why, in thousands of years, hadn't Europeans progressed philosophically and morally and ethically beyond monarchies, treating women like property, and destructive genocidal wars? One also wonders, why didn't Europeans develop surgery and agriculture as advanced as Natives?"
(This is part of an 'Answer' Carroll gave on the internet website *Quora*. The list he supplies of superior Native technologies can be instructive for Ayn Rand fans, etc. http://www.quora.com/Why-didnt-the-Native-Americans-ever-advance-technologically-over-thousands-of-years-while-Europe-and-Asia-advanced-dramatically/answer/Al-Carroll. Carroll teaches at Northern Virginia Community College.)

own, with an advanced philosophy of life that was at least as refined as their own, and a vision of peace, justice and human goodness that the Americans of the time, had they understood their own Declaration of Independence, and had they been the least bit self-aware or recalled the lessons of Judah, would have honored, respected, and learned from. Instead, we betrayed all our own ideals *

In destroying the American Indian, *this* is what we destroyed, *this* is what we stole from ourselves and from the world. Can we now return to the world what was taken? Can we replace what was lost? Not in full measure, no. But can America give back to the world even some small portion of the spiritual wisdom, the profound understanding of the sacredness of life, the longing for peace, and the respect for integrity and cooperation that we obliterated? Unless we attempt to meet *this* obligation, all the monetary compensation in the world, all the heartfelt apologies in the world, will just be 'quick fixes' and will mean very little.

Americans feel a great deal of pride that our nation is so unique, but most Americans gravely misunderstand in what *sense* we are unique, and in what sense we are no different from any other nation or any other people. We are going to have to free ourselves of quite a few delusions before we can recognize and understand our *true* uniqueness, before we can begin to speak intelligently, honestly, and maturely about our so-called 'exceptionalism". To paraphrase Jacob Needleman:

What makes America special is *not* its *people*.

What makes America special is its *obligation*:

an obligation to the human spirit, and to the world.[43]

There have been good and decent people throughout the ages, the entire world (not just America) has witnessed beneficence and sacrifice, hopes and dreams, stirring speeches and great accomplishments.

---

* Even though these very ideals had in fact been heavily influenced and informed by the principles of the Iroquois Confederacy of Nations.

But when we study history, all of this pales beside the unfathomable degree of suffering that human beings have inflicted on one another; the inconceivable amount of hatred and violence – often justified in the name of 'God', 'patriotism', or some other criminally misused grand ideal – that has spoiled the hearts and ruined the lives of so many of our ancestors: the endless war, the insatiable greed, the megalomania, the paranoia, even the phenomenal pettiness, to say nothing of the astounding lack of conscience (despite George Washington's exhortation to "Labor to keep in your breast that spark of celestial fire called conscience."[44])

It is in the context of this common history that the great crimes of genocide and slavery must be placed, and it is in this context that the delusion of America's moral superiority must be illuminated so that it can be objectively and honestly witnessed, atoned for, and perhaps – perhaps – transformed. Otherwise, if we are too insensitive, too narcissistic, too apathetic, or too weak or dishonest *to bear the truth*, the poisonous ongoing effects of lies, unfounded beliefs, and arrogance will continue to ruin our lives and will destroy the promise and the meaning of America.

"The earth's most explosive and pernicious evil is racism," noted Malcolm X, "the inability of God's creatures to live as One."

~

"America is false to the past," warned Frederick Douglass in the years before the Civil War, "false to the present, and solemnly binds herself to be false to the future."

> Americans! .... You boast of your love of liberty, your superior civilization…while the whole power of the nation…is solemnly pledged to support and perpetuate the enslavement of three million of your countrymen…. [Y]ou notoriously hate (and glory in your hatred), all men whose skins are not colored like your own.[45]

Our ancestors' shameful brutality toward African people and indigenous American people can serve to remind us that we *all* share the same inner human condition, we are all capable of barbarity and stupidity, we are all imperfect.

Fortunately, the imperfect men at the Constitutional Convention knew that this was what they had to contend with. They knew we all like to imagine that we are *only* good, just and noble, but are in fact also filled with contradictions and negativity, and are quite capable of vindictiveness and viciousness. Our national history bears unequivocal witness to this.* "The existence of slavery in this country," noted Douglass just sixty years after the convention, "brands your republicanism as a sham, your humanity as a base pretense, and your Christianity as a lie."[46]

But then Douglass added something else:

> But I differ from those who charge this baseness on the framers of the Constitution of the United States. It is a slander upon their memory....[47]

What did he mean by this?

The Hope of America

James Madison, the principal author of the Constitution, understood that strife was inevitable: people will argue and disagree about many things, and this strife must be handled to avert violence in a society. "Among the numerous advantages promised by a well-constructed Union," he wrote

---

* From genocide, to slavery and racism, to injecting citizens with syphilis, to turning away refugees fleeing Nazi Germany, to nuclear bombs, to Viet Nam, to Nicaragua, to Guantanamo, to Iraq, to drones, to violence and discrimination against immigrants, gays, women, and many others, to the mistreatment of our veterans, to the stories (from just a few days before I wrote this) about Americans seething with so much rage, fear, and hatred, that they hurled cruel insults and curses in the faces of children fleeing bloody violence from drug wars in Central America, thus bringing shame on our entire nation.

in *The Federalist Papers: No. 10*, "none deserves to be more accurately developed than its tendency to break and control the violence of faction."[48] Otherwise, "instability, injustice, and confusion" become "mortal diseases."

> By a faction I understand a number of citizens, whether amounting to a majority or minority of the whole, who are united and actuated by some common impulse of passion, or of interest, adverse to the rights of other citizens, or to the permanent and aggregate interests of the community."[49]

One possible way to eliminate "the mischiefs of faction", he noted, would be to *destroy its underlying cause*: i.e., the liberty that allows people to form their own opinions. This cure, however, would be worse than the disease. "Liberty is to faction what air is to fire," he wrote, but liberty is essential and it would make no more sense to eliminate liberty than to eliminate air.

A second potential way to solve the problem of strife among factions would be *to give all citizens the same opinions, passions, and interests.* But this is impossible. "As long as the reason of man continues fallible, and he is at liberty to exercise it, different opinions will be formed."

> The latent causes of faction are thus sown in the nature of man; and we see them everywhere brought into different degrees of activity, according to the different circumstances of civil society. A zeal for different opinions concerning religion, concerning government, and many other points… have, in turn divided mankind into parties, inflamed them with mutual animosity, and rendered them much more disposed to vex and oppress each other than to cooperate for their common good.[50]

Thus we see that Madison understood us quite well: "So strong is this propensity of mankind to fall into mutual animosities that where no substantial occasion presents itself the most frivolous and fanciful distinctions have been sufficient to kindle their unfriendly passions and excite their most violent conflicts."[51]

Fortunately, there is a third way. Madison realized that the only relief that is possible must lie in *controlling the effects* of factions: i.e., *harmonizing* the strife of inevitable opposing forces. Establishing a government and a way of life that could control the negative effects of disagreements among citizens with diverse beliefs, goals, and interests – without destroying liberty, but actually *fostering* individual freedom – was the aim of Madison and the other founders.

In fact, they hoped to create a political climate where interactions among opposing factions might even be *transforming*, might even help people to *broaden* their views. Emerson would later speak of this (threefold) phenomenon and say, "In all conversation between two persons, tacit reference is made to a third party, to a common nature.... And so in groups where debate is earnest, and especially on high questions, the company becomes aware that the thought rises to an equal level in all bosoms.... They all become wiser than they were."[52]*

~

The ideal of *freedom* that America stands for is not merely license to 'do whatever one feels like', and it is not merely the negative 'freedom from' being told what to do. Nor is it merely the freedom to get and spend and satisfy any and every mundane desire of the body. The freedom that most mattered to the founders, and that ought to matter most to all of us, is the freedom of the *mind:* a mind unconstrained by the religious, philosophical or political beliefs of others, the freedom to form one's own ideas and beliefs, the freedom to pursue what is good, meaningful, and true, the

---

* It is a sad tragedy, but hopefully only a temporary one, that this wisdom has been lost on most of our contemporary contentious government officials, as well as many people throughout the nation.

freedom (to once again use Emerson's words) to pursue "wisdom, and power, and beauty".

The ideal of *equality* that America stands for is not synonymous with 'sameness', it is not a force for leveling everyone down to the lowest common denominator, nor is it merely the right of everyone to go shopping and obtain the same 'stuff'. Equality means protecting and encouraging everyone's chance to pursue what is best and highest in themselves, to find what brings them the most genuine happiness, to have every possibility for worldly achievement and inner achievement.

The founders' work means little if some Americans are not free to pursue their dreams.

In slaughtering the American Indian, in perpetuating slavery, we denied the meaning and the possibilities of the Declaration of Independence and the Constitution, and in so doing we slandered ourselves, we denied what is best in ourselves, in our country, and in the world.

In Christian terminology, this sort of denunciation of everything that is good, noble and true, is called the "blasphemy against the Holy Spirit", and it is said to be the one "unforgivable sin". Even if we prefer not to speak in religious terms, it is difficult not to see that there is something profoundly foul in this denial. In fact, neither the horrific atrocity of slavery, nor the sickening murder of the American Indian, nor any of the horrible worldly acts we have been guilty of, are more loathsome than *the denial that we can do better*, the denial that our highest ideals *can* be fulfilled, the denial that human beings can, like Judah, become something better than what we are today. Whether by pridefully or lazily *refusing to consider* the possibility that we can do better, or by slipping into self-contempt, apathy or meaninglessness so that we *lose hope* of ever doing better – this is unforgivable.

It is unforgivable because America was consciously designed specifically as a place where ideals like freedom and equality, justice and truth, could be pursued, where the quest for "the Good" would be encouraged.

America was created as a place where all human beings could gather together and this pursuit would be protected. This is what makes America special and unique. We are no different than any other people in any other time or any other country – but no other nation has ever had this obligation to the human spirit.

The indisputable fact that we have often betrayed these ideals is not a reason to reject the ideals themselves, nor is it a reason to give up hope in the possibility of fulfilling these ideals in the future. This is why Douglass said, "But I differ from those who charge this baseness on the framers of the Constitution of the United States. It is a slander upon their memory." He did not want us ever to forget what we *are* or what we have *done*, but he also did not want us ever to forget what America can and must *become*.

It seems to be a matter of principle among some conservatives to look at any forward-looking endeavor (whether a proposed bill in Congress, or simply a suggested action that might improve some problem or other), and to search for possible difficulties or defects that might result in part. This could be a very useful thing to do. But as soon as they find one, rather than suggesting ways to modify or improve the endeavor so as to make it *more* useful and effective, they choose instead to use what they have found as a justification to condemn the entire enterprise and try to defeat it, insisting that it is always better to do nothing at all and just leave the *status quo* alone. There is always good reason to carefully consider consequences and to not rush ahead carelessly and brazenly, but I see no evidence that the extremist refrain "do nothing, the market will take care of all our problems as long as we do nothing" has any logical, historical, or moral validity.

The American experiment is just that – an ongoing experiment. This experiment does not need uncritical, unquestioning, mindless 'loyalty'. Rather, it demands our continuous efforts to advance our fundamental principles and improve the lives of all our citizens. It demands an attitude, in John Kennedy's words, that "welcomes new ideas without rigid reactions."[53] Barack Obama got it right on the 50th anniversary of the historic events in Selma, Alabama (more than 150 years after the time of Frederick Douglass), when he said: "What greater expression of faith in the American experiment than this; what greater form of patriotism is there; than the belief that America is not yet finished, that we are strong enough to be self-critical, that each successive generation can look upon our imperfections and decide that it is in our power to remake this nation to more closely align with our highest ideals."

The experiment, the pursuit of 'the Good', continues. It is a lie and a slander to deny the essential unfulfilled goodness in America, just as it is a lie and a slander to deny the essential unfulfilled goodness in oneself and all people.

~

And by all people I mean *all* people. Thankfully, as our experiment moves forward, the centuries of cruel and ignorant rhetoric about a 'homosexual agenda', the fear and hatefulness expressed by angry thugs and pretentious moralists (who time and again are found to be suppressing their own inner desires), and all the ugly physical and verbal abuse aimed at fellow human beings who happen not to share someone's holier-than-thou definition of 'normalcy', appear at last to be dwindling: though not yet completely disappearing. Gay citizens are more socially accepted than ever, but vicious anti-gay forces of discrimination and bigotry are still hard at work and gay children still live in fear, wondering why they are hated, bullied, and made fun of, wondering if they will ever truly feel safe, wondering if they will ever be allowed to live with dignity and free from contempt.

At the core of the many ignorant beliefs about homosexuality are the blind assumptions that it could *never* happen in *my* family, and that being gay is a *choice*. In fact, it can 'happen' in *any* family – and there are precious few families that won't find a gay relative somewhere in front of their noses if they only open their eyes and look. And the absurd insistence that being gay is a 'choice' is based on nothing more than wishful thinking and an insistence on believing what one wants to believe, despite all logic and evidence. The characteristics of being gay show up at a very young age, long before a child is interested in making any sort of rebellious 'choice', long before they even know what 'being gay' *is*. There are clearly genetic contributions to sexual orientation[54], and even if it is the result of something that happens in the cellular environment (leading to epigenetic enhancement or stifling of genetic expression) *in utero* or even in early childhood, being gay is not something we 'decide' in our brains or can 'decide' to change. Being gay is no more a 'decision' than being straight. We discover our sexual identity with no decision-making on our part. Obviously a straight person can choose to perform a gay *act,* just as a gay person could always marry and perform a heterosexual act – but this doesn't change one's inner sexual nature, it doesn't change the feelings, desires and attractions that arise involuntarily. Being gay is not a character issue, an illness, or a 'bad habit'. Our sexuality is woven deeply into our being by nature, which has always included it in the grand scheme of life. It is not something we chose or could change at will, and it is wrong-headed and vindictive to suggest that anyone else can, or should.

Another core belief, of course, is the fundamentalist insistence that it is "against God's law" because "the bible says so". Indeed, *Leviticus 20:13* says that if a man has sex with another man it is an abomination and both must be put to death. Then again, *Leviticus 20:9* says that a child who curses his mother or father must be put to death, and one does not hear much outcry for the enforcement of *this* law of God. *Exodus 35:2* says that anyone who does any work whatsoever on the Sabbath must be put to death. *Deuteronomy 22:20* says that if a woman is not a virgin on her wedding night, she must be put to death. The list goes on and on. No one in their right mind, including the ancient Jewish sages and rabbis, as the Talmud makes clear, would take these barbaric legalisms literally. (For instance, "an eye for an eye", was never meant to be taken as a literal decree allowing or codifying barbaric forms of punishment. It has always been understood as a requirement for fair and equitable *financial* compensation in cases of legal damages. Far from being a barbaric statement, the rule was actually just the opposite: its intent and its effect was to *curb* much of the cruelty allowed by other ancient legal systems, where terrible retribution could often be inflicted for minor offenses, while lawbreakers with 'connections' could often get off scot-free. It meant that all punishment would thenceforward have to *fit the crime*, and could not be too severe, or out-of-proportion to the offense.) But if we must insist on being literalistic cherry-pickers, I suggest we remember the lesson learned by Judah and pick *Leviticus 19:18*: "Thou shalt not take vengeance, nor bear any grudge against the children of thy people, but thou shalt love thy neighbor as thyself."

~

It is a great pending tragedy, in my opinion, that in current-day America the economic trend is toward a new oligarchy* – which is yet another betrayal of our ideals, ourselves, and each other – as a tiny percentage of citizens become phenomenally wealthy while the vast majority are returned, once again, to a state of pre-Enlightenment serfdom. "If nothing changes." notes Nick Hanauer, "in another thirty years the top 1% will share 36-37% of income, and the bottom 50% will share 6%. That's not a capitalist economy anymore, that's a feudalist economy."[55]

---

*"In one way or another," as Bill Moyers has noted, "this is the oldest story in America: the struggle to determine whether 'we, the people' is a moral compact embedded in a political contract, or merely a charade masquerading as piety and manipulated by the powerful and privileged to sustain their own way of life at the expense of others." (http://www.tomdispatch.com/blog/175783/tomgram%3A_bill_moyers ._covering_class_war)

Hanauer's statement has been countered with the observation that in feudal economies the wealth of the nobility was unearned, and the poor had virtually no possibility of ever improving their lives, whereas in a capitalist society neither of these statements hold true. This distinction was indeed the intention of the Enlightenment agenda of bringing equal opportunity to all people, but it is absurd not to notice that this is not an accurate assessment of our actual current situation. Today's economic landscape is clearly rigged in favor of a small percentage of people who already have vast amounts of wealth (and quite often, this is inherited wealth that they by no means 'earned'). The rigging consists, among other factors, of a tax system that rewards speculators more than people who do productive work, that taxes capital gains on money people already have at a lower rate than money the average American works each day to earn (allegedly because fabulously wealthy people are the job creators, a fantasy that has never been true: jobs are created by a combination of consumer spending and small business growth and innovation, not by the ultra-wealthy or massive corporations), and then permits excessive CEO and upper-management salaries while making it difficult for unions to protect working people (for instance, by attacking employee rights through such phony euphemisms as the various so-called 'right to work' laws – which have only succeeded in causing lower wages, fewer benefits, and less job security in every state were they have been enacted – while actually encouraging employers to move operations abroad if American workers complain or demand a living wage). This is all capped off with disgracefully off-base decisions by a Supreme Court that grants corporations more rights and more protections than actual human beings, so that campaign contributions are no longer seen as donations, but have morphed into 'investments' expecting a 'return': i.e., bought-and-paid-for-politicians who will obediently pass laws to serve their owners' interests.* All of this has turned back the clock on years upon years of human progress by empowering an aristocracy while weakening everyone else.

In part, of course, this is also the result of our passively believing what we are told to believe, voting against our own interests if we vote at all, resignedly accepting it all as inevitable instead of protesting, and thus allowing our individuality and inner sanctity to be trampled on. As a result, the middle class is disappearing and more citizens are living in poverty than at any time in American history.[56] We can still put a stop to this, but we had better hurry up before it is too late. These are human-made policies, they are not inevitabilities. There is no reason why we cannot exchange these policies for policies that address the needs of *all* Americans. But this can only occur if millions of people stop listening to the lies and propaganda (that intentionally distract us by instilling fear and hatred toward poor people, minorities, and immigrants), and start raising our voices and working together to preserve democracy.

The immense disparity of income and opportunity leads to hopelessness, anger, and despair, and sooner or later these pent-up emotions will have to be expressed. There are examples of wealthy members of the "1%", such as Hanauer, noticing that violent upheaval, as a response to long-term suffering and inequity, is hardly an impossibility and is something his fellow aristocrats had best be concerned with. The great irony is that everyone, including the wealthiest Americans, would benefit from less disparity of wealth. Sustained economic growth cannot occur when the vast majority of citizens have stagnant, let alone decreasing, incomes, and are increasingly unable to spend money. Enlightencd self-interest insists that we need a less divided society, a nation of unity and cohesion rather than

---

* *Citizens United*, in my opinion, is the most disgraceful Supreme Court decision since *Dred Scott*. It is an attack on everything the founders of this nation tried to achieve on behalf of the American people, and if Congress does not overturn it, it may very well signal the end of democracy as our government becomes prey to the highest bidder.

divisiveness, bitterness, and contempt. This also has strategic implications: why would people in other countries admire, respect, or seek to emulate an America that does not take care of its own?

Action must be taken, but we should be careful to remember that governmental regulations in commerce (as in education) should protect and facilitate, not impede the work of people who know what they are doing, and not turn busybody bureaucrats into hidden backstage puppeteers with a giddy sense power to manipulate others. This does not mean there should be *no* regulations – the conservative fervor for deregulation, based on the thoughtless habit of blaming every conceivable ill on the government, has been both unwarranted and clearly detrimental. The Constitution they love to wave around *requires* that the government "promote the general welfare" and "secure the blessings of liberty" for all Americans: Establishing standards of workplace safety, preventing discrimination and harassment, mandating environmental protections, and shielding businesses and consumers from unfair business practices, etc., are precisely what the government ought to be doing for the benefit of all of us. But *excessive* regulations, and badly thought out regulations, put a chill on business growth (just as they do on the ability of schools to educate children). Regulators who know nothing about the intricacies of a business or industry (like politicians and bureaucrats who know nothing about the intricacies of a classroom) continually impose an array of rules that may be well-intentioned but typically make no sense at all, and only succeed in making things difficult or impossible, while filling lots of government drawers with unread forms that just sit there waiting for something to go wrong. The government has an obligation to support, not to stifle, creativity and growth.

Refocusing our efforts, to fund new research and upgrade infrastructure, would go a long way.

This is not a call for 'socialism', government takeover of business and industry, or taking money from rich people and giving it to poor people (though it *is* a call to halt the *real* 'redistribution of wealth' that is occurring – i.e., the taking of money from the poor and middle class, and *giving it to the rich**). The economy grows, tax revenues increase, and wealth gets distributed *naturally* (amongst owners, employees, vendors, associates, and various others), when entrepreneurial ventures succeed and the rules are fair. But poorly executed business ventures must be allowed to fail. It is one thing (and a very good thing) to create a safety net of bankruptcy protections, unemployment insurance for displaced workers, etc., but if a business cannot fail – due to government subsidies or various regulations that promote the welfare of the few but not the wider society – then creativity and intelligence will routinely be ignored or crushed. Economic stupidity then aligns itself with abusive political power, and parasitic sluggish corporations are allowed to become bigger and wealthier while blocking all challenges from their more innovative betters. These greedy, subsidy-demanding, corporate bloodsuckers are not the capitalists the Enlightenment had in mind. Creative, optimistic, risk-taking entrepreneurs are the *real* capitalists.

As Jacob learned from his swindling uncle Laban, and as Christ taught in his parables, it is *good* to increase material wealth and abundance (to be 'fruitful and multiply'), it is necessary and honorable to learn how to take care of ourselves, our families, our neighbors, our posterity. But the impulse to do this cannot come from meaningless greed or feelings of entitlement. It has to come from creativity, love, and a sense of responsibility toward ourselves and each other.

---

* Why are pharmaceuticals, internet services, and food, so expensive in America compared to the rest of the industrialized world? Why are airline tickets so expensive, even when oil prices plummet? We used to have (and enforce) antitrust laws that prevented corporate monopolies. Now, giant corporations have taken over, and we have higher prices for the many and higher profits for the few. This is a hidden redistribution of wealth from the majority of Americans to the wealthiest Americans. Economics is not a 'zero-sum game', but that does not alter these facts.

Prosperity is the goal of economics. But for society as a whole, economic prosperity must be a means to an end – and all too often we have perverted this ideal through envy and greed, making the accumulation of wealth an end in itself, making it the cold relentless motive for the decisions we make as a nation and as individuals. The result of this is the emptiness and drudgery of the human ant hill, increased poverty and misery, and ever more violence in our cities and across the world, rather than the magnificent cultural flowering of beauty, wisdom and spirit, and the pursuit of 'the Good', that was the dream of the American Founders.*

Relativism

But this is the 21st century. Do we even think there *is* such a thing as "the" Good? It has become the standard in contemporary America to believe that it is morally offensive to consider anyone's personal opinion of what is right, true, or good, to be more accurate or more valid than anyone else's personal opinion. We are taught to be 'open' to the beliefs and opinions of everyone. Everything is relative, and no decent person would question this.

The paradox here is that if we must be tolerant of *any* belief, then we must necessarily be tolerant of an *intolerant* belief. This leads to the nightmare of being unable to defend ourselves morally against any sort of evil or tyranny, which

---

* When Athens became an immensely prosperous empire during the years of the Delian League, right up until their final defeat many years later by a jealous Sparta, they basked in their Classical Period. All the great works of Greek tragedy and comedy were written during this time. Most of the great architectural works were built at this time. "Flush with wealth and at peace with Persia and Sparta, the Athenians had nothing better to do with this wealth than invest it in a massive cultural flowering of art, poetry, philosophy, and architecture." When America comes out of this long economic slump, I hope we take a lesson from this. (the quote is from Hooker, Richard, *Ancient Greece, The Athenian Empire.* http://www.wsu.edu:8080/~dee/GREECE/ATHEMP.HTM1996)

is why relativism is essentially incoherent and, in the end, morally bankrupt. (But the immorality of relativism itself is not the worst of it. What is worse, is our blasé lack of concern for what this says about our lives.)

However, there is another meaning to the word 'openness' that encourages us to use reason to seek the truth, free of the constraints imposed by previously assumed (or enforced) beliefs. This kind of freedom and openness was the concern of the American Founders: the freedom of an unencumbered mind. This is quite a different matter than the kind of 'openness' that has become the philosophical basis of today's popular culture, which really just functions as an excuse for denying reason's power altogether and thoughtlessly accepting anything and everything that happens momentarily to sway us.

The result is that this popular 'openness', which we have accepted as a great virtue, just leads to indifference. We approve of this indifference because it safely and comfortably respects everyone else's opinion, no matter how sublime or ridiculous, and it promises us in return that we can 'do whatever we want'. But the consequence is that by having no real principles of our own we become the slaves of fashion and whim, and we revere whoever or whatever is the most popular that day. Tolerance of everything leaves us weak and submissive, prepared to surrender to anything. Relativism, then, is deeply entwined with the roots of our modern sense of meaninglessness.

But listening, with a respectful and open mind, is not relativism. Responsible and mature human beings *must* make moral judgments, and should have the courage to stick by their convictions. But here is the major distinction from relativism: we have to be fully aware that our judgments are *provisional.* Only a God's judgments could be absolute, not yours or mine (and if you think He's speaking to you directly face-to-face or mouth-to-ear, get help). This is why we have to be willing to listen, to consider, to respect other people's ideas, to continually reassess our own, and to sometimes find the courage and humility to change our opinions.

Our notions of goodness and justice will vary, from human to human, and within each one of us, from time to time. But this does not mean there is no such thing as objective truth, justice, or goodness. It just means that *we* do not know what it is, and the pursuit to attain it is never finished: we always remain somewhere in between knowing nothing and knowing everything. It is true that no human-made law or theory is the absolute truth. But hopefully, if we use our hearts and minds well, our laws and theories may at least draw their validity for their temporary purpose, in their own place and time, *from* absolute truth.

Most importantly, to recognize that our judgments are provisional never means we should be morally indifferent, unwilling to take a stand, or complacent in the face of evil.

Eros and the Ladder of Love

Long ago, Plato and Socrates taught the West that our great human longings – for passionate relationships, for human achievement, for wisdom, for beauty, for immortality, for union with God – are what make human life *meaningful*. And they knew that *Eros* is the key to all of this, that *Eros* makes possible the hope for human warmth, the hope for a deep connection with life and eternity, the hope for success and happiness, the hope for an understanding of the sense and meaning of existence.

This is because *Eros*, the Greek god of Love, is not merely a sexual symbol or a funny little cherub. In the great mythology of Greece, *Eros* represents the *passionate desire for all that is good, true, just, beautiful and meaningful.* He symbolizes the driving force and motivation behind all the great discoveries of science, all great art, all great social endeavors, all the magnificent efforts of the human mind, heart, and spirit. Without *Eros,* life is dry and meaningless.

In Plato's *Symposium*, Socrates says that the mysteries of *Eros* begin in our youth, when we find ourselves passionately attracted to one beautiful girl or boy. As a result of this experience we begin to entertain beautiful new thoughts and feelings.

If we are fortunate and awake, these stirring thoughts and feelings can soon lead us to an appreciation of beauty in other forms as well, and we begin to see that the beauty of one is akin to the beauty of another, and there is something magnificent and wonderful in the essence of all this loveliness and beauty throughout nature that attracts us.

Love then leads us to discover for ourselves that the beauty of a mind is even more precious and admirable than the beauty of outward form, and we find ourselves desiring interesting friends and lovers who have character, who have beautiful souls, and together we seek to bring to birth beautiful ideas and sentiments which may improve ourselves and each other.

Thence, in our converse with beautiful minds and souls, we become conscious of the beauty which exists in living well and righteously, in observing justice, in meeting our responsibilities with honor. We begin to understand that the beauty of all of this is of one family, and personal physical beauty is but a sweet and fleeting trifle.

Eros then leads us further into deeper realms of the mind, where we discover the beauty of knowledge and science and reason, and we begin to desire the splendid loveliness of wisdom.

And then, being lured by Love to surpass the limitations of reason, we begin to contemplate Universal Beauty. No longer enslaved to the attractions of just one form of beauty, *Eros* reveals a vast sea of beauty and we find ourselves creating noble, majestic, thoughts and emotions.

Finally, having been educated by all these experiences of Love, having gradually ascended this 'Ladder of Love' and thoroughly experienced and contemplated all the many aspects of the Beautiful, *Eros* leads us forth until we suddenly behold that wondrous noetic 'Beauty' that is no longer subject to death or decay, but is pure, divine, and eternal. In this sacred communion, beholding Beauty with the awakened eye of the soul, no longer seeing mere images or relying on human reason, but actually *knowing Reality*, we become a 'friend of God' – having purified and perfected our own immortal Soul.

Socrates often said that he had no wisdom at all, that he knew nothing either beautiful or good. In Plato's *Symposium*, however, he announces that he is an expert on Love. These two statements only *appear* contradictory. Love, for Socrates, meant longing, and this state of longing is what he meant by being always *between* ignorance and wisdom, *between* ugliness and beauty, always seeking and questioning and desiring. Socrates understood *Eros*, and lived passionately and erotically, precisely because he humbly acknowledged that he knew nothing, but was always an adoring lover and seeker of beauty, goodness, and truth, just as we all ought to be.

~

But *Eros* has been badly wounded, just as the ancient myth of *Eros and Psyche* described so long ago, and he has taken wing and flown away – perhaps never to return.

And so, we cannot turn on the news without being inundated with stories, images, and accusations of men abusing women, priests abusing little boys, mothers murdering their children, girls looking for sex without love and making babies without families, boys going on killing sprees to prove their manhood and feel some sort of meaning in their lives.

We have a culture that conditions us though television, movies, music and advertising, to seek as much sex as possible without compassion or responsibility. At the same time, as David Blankenhorn writes, "the idea of 'being a man' is increasingly identified with violence, materialism, and predatory sexual behavior. I am a man because I will hurt you if you disrespect me. I am a man because I have sex with lots of women and my girlfriends have babies. I am a man because I have more money and more things than you do."[57] But the standard of good fatherhood – *I am a man* *because I cherish my wife, I love my children, and I take care of my family* – does not enter into the equation.*

All of this is a twisted perversion of *Eros*. Without a higher vision guiding the mind, the heart is easily defiled, callousness and cruelty become the norm, and the longing for money and possessions, meaningless sex, and destructive power over others, replaces the lost longing for love, truth, beauty, and real joy.

So it is perhaps not surprising that the U.S. is inundated with hate groups, despite the fact that 'loving our neighbor' has been the central teaching of every one of our traditions:

> *"Do unto others as you would have them do unto you," Christ says in the Gospels,*
> *Confucius once said, "Never impose on others what you would not choose for yourself."*[58]
> *An Egyptian papyrus from 600 BCE says, "That which you hate to be done to you, do not do to another."*[59]
> *The Greek pre-Socratic philosopher, Thales, wrote, "Avoid doing what you would blame others for doing."*[60]
> *In the ancient Hindu 'Mahabharata' we find the words, "One should never do that to another which one regards as injurious to one's self."*[61]
> *One of Mohammad's sayings was, "That which you want for yourself, seek for mankind."*[62]
> *And Rabbi Hillel, a contemporary of Jesus, said, "That which is hateful to you, do not do to your fellow. That is the whole Torah; the rest is explanation."*[63]

---

* Despite good intentions, a great failing of the welfare system is the discouragement of strong families, particularly through the degradation of fathers by making welfare payments dependent on the *absence* of a working father in the home. This eliminates a breadwinner, takes away added emotional support for children, and perhaps most grievously it eliminates a positive male role model for sons. "The first priority of any serious program against poverty," George Gilder believes, and I certainly think he has a point, "is to strengthen the male role in poor families." (*Wealth and Poverty*)

All our traditions are aware that the real secret to life is loving and sharing with others. But our hearts are estranged from love, our souls have lost the guiding light of *Eros*, and we have forgotten that we are each other's keeper. This fragmentation of our inner and outer worlds inevitably leads to what the great poet, William Butler Yeats, described a century ago:

> *Things fall apart; the centre cannot hold;*
> *Mere anarchy is loosed upon the world,*
> *The blood-dimmed tide is loosed, and everywhere*
> *The ceremony of innocence is drowned;*
> *The best lack all conviction, while the worst*
> *Are full of passionate intensity.*[64]

This rupture, the broken soul directed earthward and the fleeing of *Eros*, leads to all the barbarism of today. The Mind becomes obsessed with heartless rationality, reason becomes a tyrant, and scientists begin to accumulate data-without-meaning like squirrels gathering nuts; the Heart becomes obsessed with obscenity, fear and hatred; the Body's cravings masquerade as the heart's longing; and love is analyzed and belittled by the logical positivists, deconstructionists, and all the other champions of meaninglessness. The rulers of the world "degenerate into shopkeepers in a universal assembly line,"[65] churning out mediocre goods for a debased humanity. The once living universe, filled with passion and informed by Divinity, becomes a dead mechanical universe, filled with violence and informed by the void. If *Eros* does not return, it is probably the end of the road. We will continue to demean and corrupt ourselves and each other for a little while longer, until eventually no light is left or even remembered.

But it does not have to be so. No matter how empty, hopeless, or violent life becomes, a return to meaning, wisdom, and love, is always possible. There has perhaps never been a more debased state of humanity than what was endured in the Nazi concentration camps, yet even there,

128

according to survivor Victor Frankl, one could be stronger than one's conditions. "The experiences of camp life show that man does have a choice of action."

> Man *can* preserve a vestige of spiritual freedom, of independence of mind, even in such terrible conditions of psychic and physical stress.... [E]verything can be taken from a man but one thing: the last of the human freedoms – to choose one's attitude in any given set of circumstances, to choose one's own way.[66]

Isaac and Ishmael

I began this chapter on "my brother's keeper" with a biblical tale about two brothers, Joseph and Judah, and will conclude it with a tale of two other biblical brothers, Isaac and Ishmael, whose ancient conflict (which was never their fault) is still being played out so horribly and foolishly in today's world.

Little is actually said in the Bible about Isaac. The most well-known story is the one about his near-sacrifice by his father Abraham on Mt. Moriah. In the Islamic tradition, the same story is told, but it is said that Abraham's first son, Ishmael (the ancestor of Mohammad), was the son who was nearly sacrificed. We can argue to the end of our days about the historical veracity of these two competing claims, but this is beside the point. Both stories are symbolic representations of the same profound psychological and spiritual processes that occur deep within the human soul at a certain point in its journey of awakening, and in this sense both stories are equally true. (We have to stop reducing the vast meaning and awesome power of symbolism and mythology to mere questions of literal fact or fiction. Myths reflect back to us, and teach us about, our deepest psychological and spiritual truths. Among contemporary people, myths tend to be dismissed, at a terrible psychological cost, as childish fantasies or the unscientific gropings of primitive minds. This is why followers of western religions have typically insisted that *their* scriptures are not myths at all, but must be taken as literally true. This, however, merely weakens the effectiveness and power of religions, rendering them spiritually useless, often rather foolish and open to mockery, as well as socially and politically dangerous – rather than instructive, helpful, and even ennobling.)

In the Hebrew story, God had several times promised Abraham and Sarah that their descendants would be as numerous as the stars. But when they were approaching one hundred years of age, they still had not had a child. Sarah had an Egyptian handmaiden named Hagar who, according to several tales in the Talmud, was an Egyptian Princess, a daughter of Pharaoh, who gave her to Sarah in an earlier story as a gift. Because Sarah was barren, she told Abraham to "Consort with my maid; perhaps I shall have a son through her." The girl had been raised by Sarah, and was a righteous devotee of the Lord, and thus a suitable companion for Abraham. This was a customary practice of the times (to get value from the story we can set aside for the moment our different modern definition of fidelity, and remember that this is a mythological tale from another culture).

So Abraham cohabited with Hagar and she conceived. But no sooner did Hagar realize that she was pregnant with Abraham's child, the Bible tells us, than she began to act as if the status of the two women had been reversed, and she began to treat her mistress scornfully.

An angry Sarah blamed Abraham. "The wrong done me is your fault! I myself put my maid in your bosom; now that she sees that she is pregnant, I am lowered in her esteem. The Lord decide between you and me!" But Abraham simply said, "Your maid is in your hands. Deal with her as you think right." The miffed Sarah then began to treat Hagar harshly, and the handmaiden ran away.

*When Hagar ran away, God sent an angel to speak to her.
The angel found her at a desert spring near Kadesh [a*

word which means 'Holy']. "Hagar," said the angel,
"where have you come from, and where are you going?"
Hagar answered, "I am running away from my cruel
mistress." The angel then told her that she must return and
endure her, but he also made known to her that she would
be the mother of a race of great warriors. "You shall bear
a son and name him 'Ishmael', which means 'God heeds',*
for the Lord has heeded your suffering." Hagar cried,
"The Lord has seen me!", and she named the well
Beer-lahai-roi, [which means] 'the well of the Living One
who sees me'. (Gen.16.7-14)

When Ishmael was thirteen years old, Sarah at last gave
birth to her own son, Isaac. More trouble soon ensued.

Sarah saw the son whom Hagar the Egyptian had
borne to Abraham playing. She said to Abraham,
"Cast out that slave-woman and her son, for the
son of that slave shall not share in the inheritance
with my son Isaac." The matter distressed
Abraham greatly, for it concerned a son of his. But
God said to Abraham, "Do not be distressed over
the boy or your slave; whatever Sarah tells you, do
as she says, for it is through Isaac that offspring
shall be continued for you. As for the son of the
slave-woman, I will make a nation of him, too,
for he is your seed." (Gen.21.9-13)

So Abraham obeyed Sarah, he prepared water and bread
for Hagar and the boy, and sadly sent them off.
When the water ran out, Hagar burst into tears and
walked away from Ishmael: she could not bear to see him
die. But God heard the boy and sent an angel to reassure
them. "Come", he said to Hagar, "lift up the boy and hold
him by the hand, for I will make a great nation of him."

---

* Ishmael is described by the angel as a powerful warrior and a great
chieftain who will thrive in the wilderness.

Then God opened her eyes and she saw a well of
water. She went and filled the skin with water, and
let the boy drink. God was with the boy and he
grew up; he dwelt in the wilderness and became a
bowman. He lived in the wilderness of Paran
[meaning 'Beauty' or 'Glory']. (Gen.21.19-21)

So Ishmael, too, is to have a share in God's Covenant
with Abraham: he too will give birth to a great nation. His
father Abraham loved him[*], and when the time came for the
boy to depart, he provided him with bread (spiritual
sustenance) and water (spiritual truth). And when this ran
out, God *Himself* appeared and gave him *more*: the Lord
'opened Hagar's eyes' – that is, He opened the Eye of her
Soul, so that she could '*see*' the Truth and convey it to her
son. Ishmael, we are told, drank this 'water', and he went on
to live in Beauty and Glory.

~

Years later, immediately after the near-sacrifice, the
Bible tells us that Sarah passed away. When the time of
mourning was over, Abraham sent his servant to the land of
his birth to find a wife for Isaac. The servant brought ten
camels laden with gifts, and when he arrived outside the city
he stopped beside a well and prayed for a sign. Instantly the
beautiful Rebecca appeared, who turned out to be the
granddaughter of Abraham's brother Nahor, and she
possessed a generous and loving nature much like Abraham
himself. Rebecca agreed to return with Abraham's servant
and marry Isaac.

Just as Rebecca reached the home of Abraham, we learn
that "Isaac had just come back from the vicinity of Beer-
lahai-roi", which means 'the well of the Living One who

---

[*] Legends in the Jewish Oral Tradition, preserved in the Talmud, tell us
that Abraham visited his beloved elder son on many occasions
throughout his life. According to Islam, during one of these visits
Abraham and Ishmael together built the *Ka'bah*, the great Sanctuary in
Mecca.

sees me', and was so named many years earlier by Hagar. "Isaac then brought her into the tent of his mother Sarah, and he took Rebecca as his wife. Isaac loved her, and thus found comfort after his mother's death."

In the very next sentence the Bible tells us that Abraham also now remarried, this time to a woman named Keturah, and they had several children. Before he died, he gave these children many gifts, and sent them "to the land of the East." Abraham lived to be one hundred and seventy-five years old, and then "breathed his last, dying at a good ripe age, old and contented, and he was gathered to his kin." Isaac and Ishmael buried him in the cave of Machpelah. After this, we are told, "Isaac settled near Beer-lahai-roi." The episode ends with a summary of the posterity of Ishmael, all of whom "camped alongside all their kinsmen."

This perplexing medley of information begins to sort itself out and make sense when we learn from the oral tradition that 'Keturah' was another name for Hagar ('Keturah' means *perfumed*, and it is said in the Jewish tradition that Hagar was 'perfumed with good deeds'). Before Rebecca arrived, Isaac had been in Beer-lahai-roi – which strongly suggests he had been with Hagar and his brother Ishmael. Evidently the brothers' influence brought Hagar and Abraham back together again after the death of Sarah. Abraham lived another thirty-seven years and had many more children, as did Ishmael, and this formerly divided family lived all together once again, everyone "alongside all their kinsmen". When Abraham passed away, Isaac and Ishmael brought him home and buried him with Sarah, and then Isaac returned to the family and "settled near Beer-lahai-roi."

This story speaks to us on many levels. On a psychological and family level, it suggests that it is never too late for broken families to come back to each other and heal their wounds. Spiritually and symbolically, the story reminds us that the various inner forces within the soul, no matter how divergent, can still reunite and work together in a state of harmony. But most importantly for our consideration today, on a social and political level, given the immense importance of this particular family for all of western history, it clearly tells us that since Isaac and Ishmael could reunite as brothers, there is no reason why their children, Jews and Muslims, cannot do the same.[67]

CHAPTER SEVEN

BEYOND RELIGIOUS TOLERANCE

In late January, 2012, a young man was arrested in Paramus, NJ, for firebombing two Synagogues. One of his Molotov cocktails ignited a fire in the second-floor bedroom of the Rabbi, who lived with his family above the synagogue. They were all sleeping at the time. The police confirmed that the perpetrator knew people were in the residence, and "the arson and attempted murder were a direct result of his hatred of people of the Jewish faith."

He wasn't alone. In the same month, another man launched his own Molotov-cocktail attacks on a Mosque in Queens. He later told police he intended to "kill as many Muslims and Arabs as possible."

It would be tedious and unnecessary to look at all these sorts of stories. But it is important to acknowledge the reality of hate crimes in America, and not delude ourselves into believing that racial, religious, and other forms of hatred, discrimination and violence, have disappeared. In fact, the number of Hate Groups in the U.S. increased each year during the first decade of the new millennium, from 602 in 2000 to a peak of 1,018 in 2011, according to reports from the Southern Poverty Law Center, which monitors such groups.[68] The good news is that during the following three years the number of these groups decreased, to 'only' 874 by 2014. (Part of this drop in numbers is attributed to a strengthening economy and much greater public distaste for those promoting openly racist, and other hateful, views. Unfortunately, another part is attributed to people leaving those groups for the safety, anonymity, and greater reach for their invective that can be achieved on the Internet. More than half of the decrease is attributable to Ku Klux Klan chapters, a large number of which are suspected of having gone underground rather than actually disbanding.) Sadly, in 2015. The number rose again, back to 998. "Antigovernment militiamen, white supremacists, abortion foes, domestic Islamist radicals, neo-Nazis and lovers of the Confederate battle flag targeted police, government officials, black churchgoers, Muslims, Jews, schoolchildren, Marines, abortion providers, members of the Black Lives Matter protest movement, and even drug dealers."[69]

Extremists, of any faith or culture share this essential quality: they discount the basic humanity of whole populations of people, whom they depict with ignorant stereotypes. This is never innocent or harmless. What happens when an entire population's humanity is denied? In World War II we got the Holocaust. In late 19th and early 20th century America, we got thousands of lynchings of young black men. In Europe, in the 1990's, we got Christian Serbs raping somewhere between 12,000 and 50,000 Muslim women and young girls (justified as an "effective tool" of warfare, but clearly a use of terror as part of their program of ethnic cleansing). On 9/11, we got the attacks on the Twin Towers and the Pentagon.

The great public narrative of our post-9/11 lives is that we are engaged in a War on Terror, a great battle between cosmic forces of Good and Evil. No rational person can deny that groups like al-Qaeda and ISIS are threatening civilization with wholesale destruction, and their barbarity and cruelty must be resisted and defeated. This was the lesson that Krishna taught Arjuna long ago in the *Bhagavad Gita:* sometimes one must do one's duty, sometimes one must stand up for what is right and fight against evil, sometimes one must simply do what has to be done – even when this includes fighting or even killing. But Krishna also taught Arjuna that this is not to be done with a heart full of hatred, arrogance, or anger, but consciously and from a place of love, with no attachment to the outcome, without greedily wishing for vengeance or reward. It is not to be done for our own self-aggrandizement or to feed our ego's illusions of superiority, but for a higher good, always remembering that there is infinitely more to the world than what we can see or understand. Similarly, when Christ taught his disciples to love their enemies, he was not being naïve, and he was not telling them to be docile. Like Krishna, he was teaching them that whatever has to be done must always be done with one's heart in the right place. Of course we must protect ourselves and each other, but an 'us-vs-them' mentality, fueled by fear, hatred, pride, and exaggerated stereotypes, will only prolong the horror. How many ages of bloodshed must pass before we see how useless this is, and how wise the words of Christ and Krishna really are?

The day after the 9/11 attack, police on Long Island had to arrest a man who was trying to run down an innocent Pakistani woman with his car. He kept shouting "I'm doing this for my country." A few days later, someone opened fire and killed a man in an Arizona Gas Station, because the man was wearing a Turban. The man was a Sikh, the follower of a religion that developed on the Indian sub-continent, and has nothing to do with Islam or al-Qaeda.

Fortunately, there were also other kinds of responses following the attack. After hearing the news that morning, neighbors of a small Islamic school in a non-Muslim neighborhood in Seattle placed flowers by the school entrances and a note that read "Not all Americans blame all Muslims". During the following months, neighbors volunteered and took turns standing watch by the school, twenty-four hours a day, to make sure there were no violent backlash incidents, particularly since they might have endangered children.

In Virginia, after vandals defaced a Mosque on the night of September 11th by spray painting "Kill the Muslims" and various obscenities on its walls and front sign, neighbors came together to help them clean up. A Jewish neighbor offered to buy the Mosque a new sign.

Throughout America, multi-Faith services were held – including services at National Cathedral and Yankee Stadium. As Cardinal McCarrick, the Catholic Archbishop of Washington, said at one of these services, "I think it is important to put our arms around our Muslim brothers and sisters right now, so they know we love them, and know we care." Cardinal McCarrick's words point to the kind of men and women of character that we *can be*.

One thing these stories suggest is that it is easy to feel hatred toward complete strangers who we can label as "other" or "different", but it is far more difficult to belittle and kill a person you know, a person with whom you have shared experiences, a person who has been your neighbor and friend.

If we could extend this idea, the way ethical teachings from all our traditions advise – and not just love the neighbor next door, but extend the concept of 'neighbor' to our fellow human beings around the world – much human misery would quickly come to an end. Easier said than done. But in our ever-shrinking global community, with rapid transportation, social media, cell phones, and multinational business, we are presented with possibilities for neighborliness, closeness and peace that the planet has never experienced before. Getting to know another person is the main remedy for stereotyping. It is not a silver bullet, but it certainly helps mitigate the fear and distrust among strangers that is the driving force behind so much hatred and violence.

In late May, 2015, for instance, some 250 armed, angry, anti-Muslim protestors descended on a Mosque in Phoenix, AZ, at the time of their evening prayers. They carried signs and wore T-shirts emblazoned with obscene and hateful anti-Muslim comments. (A counter-demonstration, with approximately the same number of demonstrators, also gathered at the Mosque, and the two sides exchanged insults and taunts.) Usama Shami, president of the Islamic center, rather than meeting hate with hate, quietly invited the anti-Muslim protestors to come inside and join them in their prayers. Most of course refused, but some did accept the invitation. One such guest noted with surprise that he was made to feel welcome by a room full of peaceful people. He then acknowledged that too many people say things out of anger that they don't even really believe: this experience, he said, changed him. Another shook people's hands before leaving, and promised them that he would never again put on the T-shirt he was wearing. Shami told the *Washington Post:* "A lot of them, they've never met a Muslim, or they haven't had interactions with Muslims. A lot of them are filled with hate and rage. Maybe they went to websites that charged them with this hatred. So when you sit down and talk like rational people, without all these slogans, without being bigots, without bringing guns, they will find out that they're talking to another human."[70]

~

Given the way the lines have been drawn in our contemporary world, it can be illuminating to recall where the very concept of 'religious tolerance' came from. It was not conceived in America, or England, or Europe. It does not come from ancient Greece, and it is not a gift to humankind from Christianity or Judaism.

We owe the invention of religious tolerance to Iran.

It was a long time ago. It was called 'Persia' at the time. But 'Persia' is 'Iran'. In 539 BCE, King Cyrus the Great of Persia conquered Babylonia. This was the time of the Babylonian Exile, when surviving Jewish tribes from Jerusalem, as well as many other people from many other places, had been taken captive and brought to Babylon. Cyrus now became the new ruler of Babylon, and on a cylinder – which was the usual place to write things down at the time – Cyrus wrote a chronicle of his battles and his royal decrees. This cylinder still exists: it is on display in the British Museum.

His decrees can be paraphrased into three major categories: (1) Racial, linguistic, and religious equality were official policies of the Empire; (2) Slaves and all captured peoples were to be allowed to return to their homes; (3) All destroyed Temples were to be restored.

This was the world's first charter of human rights.

Ever since, there have been objections to promoting religious tolerance. For instance, one objection is that taking a position of tolerance is only about being 'nice', in a sentimental and condescending way: a pretense to help us 'put up' with other people – even though we are absolutely certain that we are 'right' and they are 'wrong', and even if we really can't stand them. Thus, the whole thing is just a politically correct hypocritical lie.

Something more than being 'nice' *is* needed. Something more than 'mere tolerance' is needed, something much more significant than simply a 'live and let live' philosophy. Avoiding fistfights is fine, but then what? There is nothing here from which to construct anything positive or lasting. Mere tolerance is a low hurdle to clear, and it can easily be cleared without having to give up any of our hatred, our arrogance or our ignorance about the people we are condescendingly tolerating.

Another objection is that religious tolerance means we shall have to give up our love and passion for what we believe to be most right and true, most unique, and most sacred about our own faith tradition, and will have to water everything down so we can all be the 'same', or come to some sort of consensus about a bland, inoffensive, new religion that we can all convert to.

But that is not the point at all. On the contrary, we need to respect, learn about, and even celebrate our religious *differences*, we need to appreciate all this rich diversity – and stop using it as a justification for puffing ourselves up with pride, and feeling the need to beat other people over the head who disagree with us. Sometimes feeling offended is the price we pay for living in a pluralistic society – disputes will occur. But despite all the blustering rhetoric of the past few years, in Washington and throughout so much of the American conversation, disagreement does not require defamation, nor does it require the questioning of anyone's patriotism, moral worth, or right to exist.

Religious Tolerance in America

The idea of religious tolerance can be found in the writings of John Locke, one of the great philosophical forebears of our way of life. In his *'Letter on Tolerance'*, published in London in 1689, he presented two revolutionary ideas: (1) That religion is a matter of individual choice, not the decision of the state or the community; and (2) If you don't approve of your neighbor's choices, too bad. Live and let live and keep the peace.

Somewhat later, on this side of the Atlantic, the great American thinker, Thomas Paine, would take issue with Locke. Paine well knew that Locke's form of tolerance carried the taint of condescension, as if it were a 'gift' that the powerful could bestow upon the 'less worthy' – and which they could just as easily take away.

Paine would have none of this, and neither should we – though this is what many people think tolerance is about. Locke's type of tolerance, Paine wrote in his book *The Rights of Man*, is "not the opposite of intolerance, but it is the counterfeit of it. Both are despotisms. The one assumes to itself the right of withholding Liberty of Conscience, and the other [assumes to itself the right] of granting it."[71] Paine dedicated his book to George Washington, who agreed with him. No religion in America, Washington insisted, was to be privileged. "It is now no more that toleration is spoken of," he wrote in a letter in 1790, "as if it was by the indulgence of one class of people that another enjoyed the exercise of their inherent natural rights. For happily the Government of the United States, which gives to bigotry no sanction, to persecution no assistance, requires only that they who live under its protection, should demean themselves as good citizens."[72]

Of course, many people assume that when Washington, and other Founders, said things like this, they were really only talking about freedom of religion among various *Christian sects*. After all, they knew little or nothing about other religions and were not including them.

This assumption is false.

Washington's letter, quoted above, was written to a Jewish congregation in Newport, RI.

Thomas Jefferson, writing about the *Virginia Act for Religious Freedom*, says in his *Autobiography* that the bill was "meant to comprehend, within the mantle of its protection, the Jew and the Gentile, the Christian and Mohammedan, the Hindu and ... every denomination."[73]

James Madison, the principal author of the Constitution as well as the First Amendment, had earlier protested a proposed Virginia bill that would have used taxpayer money to pay Christian Clergy: "Who does not see that the same authority which can establish Christianity, in exclusion of all other Religions, may establish with the same ease any particular sect of Christians, in exclusion of all other sects?"[74]

So clearly, the founders were well aware of religions besides Christianity.

Even so, another assumption insists that nonetheless the founders themselves were practicing Christians, much like contemporary American Christians.

This assumption, too, is false.

According to one of Benjamin Franklin's closest friends, Rev. Joseph Priestly (the chemist and co-discoverer of oxygen, as well as a minister), "It is much to be lamented that a man of Franklin's general good character and great influence should have been an unbeliever in Christianity, and also to have done as much as he did to make others unbelievers."[75]

Thomas Paine would write, "I do not believe in the creed professed by the Jewish Church, by the Roman Church, by the Greek Church, by the Turkish Church, by the Protestant Church, nor by any Church that I know of. My own mind is my own church. Each of those churches accuse the other of unbelief; and for my own part, I disbelieve them all."[76]

There is no mention anywhere of Christianity or Jesus in the extensive correspondence of George Washington. Historian Barry Schwartz writes: "Washington's practice of Christianity was limited and superficial because he was not himself a Christian.... He repeatedly declined the church's sacraments. Never did he take communion, and when his

wife, Martha, did, he waited for her outside the sanctuary....
Even on his deathbed, Washington asked for no ritual,
uttered no prayer to Christ, and expressed no wish to be
attended by His representative."[77]

But these men, for the most part, were not atheists.
America's founders were mostly *Deists*: a spiritual
philosophy which holds that Reason, and observation of the
Natural World, without any need for organized religion,
shows us that the universe is the product of a divine Creator
– but one who rarely, if ever, intervenes in earthly affairs,
and with whom (in complete contradistinction to a primary
tenet of Christianity) we have *no personal relationship*. This
is why Jefferson's Declaration of Independence never
mentions Jesus Christ or Christianity, but does attribute
humanity's self-evident rights and equality to "the Laws of
Nature and Nature's God."

At a young age, Franklin tells us, "Some books against
Deism fell into my hands. . . It happened that they wrought
an effect on me quite contrary to what was intended by them;
for the arguments of the Deists, which were quoted to be
refuted, appeared to me much stronger than the refutations;
in short, I soon became a thorough Deist."[78]

In *Washington and Religion,* Paul F. Boller, Jr., writes:
"Washington had an unquestioning faith in Providence and
he voiced this faith publicly on numerous occasions. ...
There is every reason to believe, from a careful analysis of
religious references in his private correspondence, that
Washington's reliance upon a Grand Designer along Deist
lines was as deep-seated and meaningful for his life as, say,
Ralph Waldo Emerson's serene confidence in a Universal
Spirit permeating the ever shifting appearances of the
everyday world."[79]

Boller includes a quote from Arthur B. Bradford, an
associate of Ashbel Green (a minister who had known
Washington personally). "[Green] often said in my hearing,
though very sorrowfully of course, that while Washington
was very deferential to religion and its ceremonies, like

nearly all the founders of the Republic, he was not a Christian, but a Deist."[80]

But perhaps the most important evidence that America is not a "Christian Nation" comes from our legal documentation. To begin with, if the U.S. was founded on the Christian religion, the Constitution could clearly have said so. It does not. Nowhere in the document is there any mention of God, Jesus Christ, or Christianity. (In fact, the only mentions of the word 'religion' are in Article IV, which states that "no religious test" shall ever be required to hold office in the United States, and the First Amendment, which forbids the government from interfering with anyone's religious practice or establishing a government sponsored, required, or preferred religion.)

Even so, it would certainly be useful to have a clear, affirmative, straightforward statement, somewhere in our national documentation, that testifies one way or another as to whether the founders of this nation believed they were forming a "Christian Nation" or not.

We do have such a document.

In the final days of Washington's second term, his administration was negotiating a treaty with the nation of Tripoli. This was a common type of treaty that had to do with shipping rights and protecting free trade from piracy and other obstacles. The treaty was completed when John Adams' presidency had begun, and Adams signed it and sent it to the Senate for ratification.

Article XI of the treaty begins with this clear, blunt, unequivocal statement:

"As the Government of the United States is not, in any sense, founded on the Christian religion...."

The entire treaty was read out loud to the assembled Senate: there can be no assumption that they did not know what the document contained. They ratified it unanimously, only the third time that a Senate motion was passed unanimously with no objections from anyone. The treaty

144

was then published in full in newspapers throughout the thirteen states – this at a time when people read newspapers ravenously – and there is no record of any complaints or outrage from this first generation of proud, and informed, Americans.

In 1808, Thomas Jefferson gave a speech and said:

> Because religious belief, or non-belief, is such an important part of every person's life, freedom of religion affects every individual. State churches that …force their views on persons of other faiths undermine all our civil rights…. Erecting the "wall of separation between church and state," therefore, is absolutely essential in a free society. We have experienced…the quiet as well as the comfort which results from leaving everyone to profess freely and openly those principles of religion which are the inductions of his own reason and the serious convictions of his own inquiries.[81]

Mixing politics and religion, history has shown, is like mixing drinking and driving. And yet, a 2007 survey by the First Amendment Center found that 55 percent of Americans believe this country is "a Christian Nation." The Constitution, it goes without saying, expressly forbids any such thing. But the confusion is perhaps understandable – despite all our talk about the separation of church and state, religious language shows up in our political culture in all sorts of ways, from the Pledge of Allegiance, to phrases written on our money, to statements written on the walls of our court houses and government buildings.

But the founding fathers did not do this. It mainly began during the Great Depression in the 1930s, when business leaders found that their public prestige had plummeted and their businesses were under attack by Roosevelt's New Deal. "To regain the upper hand, corporate leaders fought back on all fronts," writes historian Kevin Kruse. "But nothing worked particularly well until they began an inspired public relations offensive that cast capitalism as the handmaiden of Christianity."[82]

Accordingly, throughout the 1930s and '40s, corporate leaders marketed a new ideology that combined elements of Christianity with an anti-federal libertarianism. Powerful business lobbies like the United States Chamber of Commerce and the National Association of Manufacturers led the way, promoting this ideology's appeal in conferences and P.R. campaigns. Generous funding came from prominent businessmen, from household names like Harvey Firestone, Conrad Hilton, E. F. Hutton, Fred Maytag and Henry R. Luce to lesser-known leaders at U.S. Steel, General Motors and DuPont.

In a shrewd decision, these executives made clergymen their spokesmen. As Sun Oil's J. Howard Pew noted, polls proved that ministers could mold public opinion more than any other profession. ...

The most important clergyman for Christian libertarianism, though, was the Rev. Billy Graham.... The Garden of Eden, he informed revival attendees, was a paradise with "no union dues, no labor leaders, no snakes, no disease." In the same spirit, he denounced all "government restrictions" in economic affairs, which he invariably attacked as "socialism."[83]

It was not until 1954 that Congress added "under God" to the previously secular Pledge of Allegiance. It also placed "In God We Trust" on postage stamps that same year, and in 1955 voted to add it to paper money (the motto had appeared briefly on coins in response to religious sentiment during the Civil War, but then disappeared by 1883 and only returned

146

to our coins in 1938). In 1956, Congress made it the nation's official motto.

Soon, many Americans were fooled into believing that their country had always been a 'Christian nation', a belief that unfortunately is now often accompanied by all sorts of preposterous pseudo-religious fantasies about Jesus and America, all of which allows demagogues and haters to whip some people up into dangerous and distorted "patriotic" frenzies.

But I hasten to add that the "wall of separation" that America's Founders deliberately constructed between the government and all religions, does not put a damper on Christianity or any other faith. It actually protects and encourages religion. It is precisely because our secular government allows the free expression of religious and non-religious ideas, with no preferences and no interference, that religion flourishes in America.

~

In 1889, Chicago was preparing for its World's Fair, and a man named Charles Bonney became concerned that leading Chicagoans were too focused on showing off humanity's *material* accomplishments, at the expense of its intellectual, artistic, and *spiritual* achievements. Something more, he insisted, was needed, and the Fair's planners agreed. They thus convened, as part of the Fair, what they called the World Parliament of Religions.

Regrettably, even as representatives from many of the world's religions came to participate and learn from each other, there were some figures who refused. The Archbishop of Canterbury strongly objected that Christianity could not be presented alongside other religions, as it alone contained Truth. The Sultan of the Ottoman Empire, Islam's Caliph, refused to send any Muslims – for precisely the same reason. (Of course, the Sultan and the Archbishop would soon have to make room for yet another claimant to infallibility, as 19th century Science put forth its claim to be not only one way of knowing truth, but the sole reliable way for knowing anything at all.)

A Presbyterian Minister, John Barrows, did attend the Parliament, and when he addressed the gathering he asked, "Why should not Christians be *glad* to learn from what God has wrought through Buddha and Zoroaster, through the Sages of China, and the Prophets of India, and the Prophet of Islam?"[84]

Rev. Barrows never changed his personal conviction that salvation can only be reached through Jesus, and he several times repeated his belief that faith in Jesus was intended for all humanity. But he showed himself capable of holding two ideas at once:

(1) a certainty about his own faith, and;

(2) at the same time, a willingness to listen respectfully to others who were equally certain of their own faiths.

Another of the speakers who did come was Vivekananda, a friend and disciple of Ramakrishna of India. Since many people had never even seen a Hindu before, thousands of people came to hear him speak. "Sectarianism," he began, "bigotry, and its horrible descendant, fanaticism, have long possessed this beautiful earth. They have filled the earth with violence, drenched it often with human blood, destroyed civilizations, and sent whole nations to despair.... But now their time has come, and I fervently hope that the bell that tolled this morning in honor of this convention may be the death-knell of fanaticism."[85]

Ramakrishna, the Hindu holy man and Vivekananda's mentor, was one of the truly great spiritual figures of the 19th century. Basic to his teachings was his conviction that religions can exist in harmony because they all lead to the same God. He delved deeply into the ideas and principles of all traditions, and seekers from many religions were drawn to his life and teachings.

He pursued Christianity, for instance, not like a modern once-a-week church-goer, but like a Desert Father, ceaselessly praying and contemplating the teachings of Jesus, while fasting and meditating alone in the woods of Panchavati. Then one day, after many months, he came out and proclaimed to his Hindu disciples, "I found God at the end of the road of Christianity. If anyone follows Christ he will reach God. I have verified it."[86]

Another time, he decided to study Islam. He had himself converted, and after studying with a Muslim teacher he again retired into the woods to contemplate what he had learned from the Qur'an. Months later he came out of seclusion and declared, "That road too leads to the same King!"[87]

Ramakrishna demonstrated, like many mystics before him and since, that the revelation and experience of God takes place at all times and is not the monopoly of any particular faith or people. Even St. Augustine would say, "That which today is called the Christian religion existed among the ancients, and has never ceased to exist from the origin of the human race…"[88]

"Religions differ," Ramakrishna once said, "in their appearance. But not in their essence. No matter which path you take it will usher you, in the end, into God's presence! Since religions are but means of finding God, why quarrel about their respective merits and defects? That will get you nowhere!"[89] This is because every religion has two aspects:

1) an outer *exoteric* aspect, which gives the masses of followers a common story to be proud of, a comforting feeling of security that God is their invisible friend who loves them and will take care of them, hope for the future, and some moral and ethical rules that are meant, at least initially, to help them keep their souls out of trouble. Unfortunately, because the outer stories and ceremonies of each religion are different, a superficial, one-sided understanding of religion tends to cause division, hatred and contempt for

149

others as well as fear of others, and this will not only lead to various forms of fundamentalism that narrow our vision and constrict our hearts, but also inevitably to violence and war;

2) an inner *esoteric* aspect (that can be revealed by reading the scriptures symbolically rather than literally), for the adepts and disciples (we are all invited), that teaches a method of attaining 'Enlightenment': i.e., the experience of Oneness with all of creation, and the return, while conscious and alive, to a state of loving communion with Divinity. This is the "essence" of religion that Ramakrishna was referring to. These *inner* teachings, as he discovered, are *always in essence the same*, which is why a deep, mature, and thorough understanding of religion can only *unite* us: after all, we are all children of the same God/Higher Power/Divine Source (the label does not matter), we are all in the same boat, we are all on the same journey, and all these paths – whether we call the journey the Return to the Promised Land, the Quest of the Holy Grail, Persephone's Return to Olympus, Mohammad's Journey to the Seven Heavens, or any other name – always lead in the end to the same destination.*

Reading these stories in a superficial, external, and literal way either leads to regressive fundamentalism, or to that contempt for religion such as one hears (with good reason!) in the sarcasm of Bill Maher or Richard Dawkins: indeed, if this version of 'religion' was all that religion consisted of, I would be the first atheist in line.

---

* Interested readers may wish to see my book on this subject, *Symbols, Meaning, and the Sacred Quest: Spiritual Awakening in Jewish, Christian, and Islamic Stories,* or my book that covers the same inner journey as it is elucidated in the Greek Myths, *Love, Wisdom, and God: The Longing of the Western Soul.*

I am suggesting instead that we revisit these stories as the deeply meaningful and instructive *myths* they were always meant to be.[*]

The different ways the stories are told, by different peoples in different times and places, attests to the marvelous range of the human imagination: the wonderful diversity in these tales should be cherished, shared, and appreciated – not abused as a reason to exclude, hate, or kill each other. Because the underlying *unity* of these stories is even more striking than their diversity: *they all lead to the same destination.* When read metaphorically, all the religions of the world remind us that we are all here for the same reason – to experience life to its fullest, to love ourselves and each other unconditionally, to open our hearts and minds to the full splendor of the universe, and to awaken that spark of divinity within each of us that can lift our soul back to its source in conscious communion. As the great Afghan poet Rumi said in the 13th century:

If people but knew their own religion . . .
how tolerant they would become.
And how free from any grudge,
against the religion of others.

Ramakrishna would agree with the great American Protestant theologian, Reinhold Niebuhr, who said we need to take religion seriously, but not literally. Niebuhr recognized that religion is an important part of life for many people, but he didn't advocate a narrow sanctimonious piety or an excuse for arrogance and divisiveness. Religion should not keep people apart – and it only does so when it is considered literally, legalistically, and politically, for this

---

[*] "Half the people in the world think that the metaphors of their religious traditions, for example, are facts. And the other half contends that they are not facts at all. As a result, we have people who consider themselves believers because they accept metaphors as facts, and we have others who classify themselves as atheists because they think religious metaphors are lies.... Which group really gets the message?" — Joseph Campbell, in *Thou Art That: Transforming Religious Metaphor.*

leads to all sorts of spiritual absurdities and social cruelties, as blind followers accept the prejudicial notions that others have told them to believe.

This sort of religion is contrary to the deepest teachings of Moses, Christ, Mohammad, and all great religious teachers, who all teach their followers to open their hearts and minds (not to close them), to be responsible, and to *learn how to think for themselves*. I know this does not sound like what many people think of when they hear the word 'religion' and assume it requires blind faith in what someone else says. But as Emerson noted, we ascribe greatness to individuals who assert their *own* truths and have the courage of their convictions. Each one of us, he added, should also "learn to detect and watch that gleam of light"[90] And this is precisely why Christ looked Pilate in the eye, when the Roman Procurator asked him if he was indeed the king of the Jews, and said "Do you ask this from yourself, or did others tell you about me?" The message for all of us is clear: *"Think for yourself, don't just believe what you've been told."*

During the Chicago Fair, a New York newspaper wrote about the various speeches and presentations, and said of Ramakrishna's disciple, Vivekananda, "He is undoubtedly the greatest figure in the Parliament of Religions. After hearing him, we feel how foolish it is to send missionaries to this learned nation." [91]

Vivekananda offered a living counterpart to a false and ugly stereotype of the 'backward Hindu'. How unfortunate that the Sultan refused to send Muslim representatives to this event back in the 1890's. How different might have been the relations of America and Islamic nations if a respectful dialogue had started back then.

But certainly we can still pursue such dialogue today. It does not require a World Parliament, just individuals and groups getting to know each other and sharing their ideas, their traditions, and their experiences. Each of us can do that, whether it's a formal meeting arranged by a Church, Synagogue, or Mosque; or a small dinner party in one's home; or just two friends hanging out.

In 2001, a Conservative Jewish congregation in Baltimore set up a program with a local Presbyterian church, to spend several weeks discussing *Genesis*. The result of these meetings was not that everyone came together in their beliefs about the meaning of the text, nor did they strike a middle ground, and no one became convinced that their own views were wrong and the other group was right. To the contrary, one Jewish member said, "The Jewish participants had their Jewish identity strengthened." [92]

After a similar event, right about the same time, that matched a group of Catholics with a group of Buddhists, a Catholic participant wrote, "It doesn't mean we're shedding one ounce of Catholic identity. I think we're expressing it to the fullest."

The Rabbi in the first group put it this way, "People tend to think this is diplomacy, that one has to convince the other, or we'll meet in the middle, or the Christians have to give up one person of the Trinity. That's not the case at all. Hopefully, no one walked away from this encounter unchanged. But that doesn't mean I'm going to give up who I am."

Instead, many participants realized that in this kind of dialogue, perhaps for the first time, you have to really think about what it is you believe, because you've got to explain it, clearly, to someone who knows little or nothing about it. At the same time, you get to listen to that other person, you get to ask questions. You get in touch with your own heritage and you gain insights from another heritage, and both spiritual identities can be *strengthened*.

In these days of divisiveness, rudeness, refusal to compromise, refusal to speak civilly to each other, and all the childish spitefulness and arrogance that pervades so much of the American conversation, we seem to have forgotten the simple and obvious fact that it is possible to understand each other, to respect each other, and even like each other, and nonetheless have profound differences.

In our ever-shrinking world, where the word 'community' means that more and more cultural and religious diversity is right beside us, we really have no choice but to find out who our neighbors are. Otherwise, we just hide from the world. This sort of isolation could be achieved in the past, but no longer in this fantastically close-knit world. Militant exclusivity, particularly in its violent forms, may make headlines – but it does not make much sense.

Islamophobia

The heavy media coverage of violent activities by small groups of Islamic terrorists helps cement in the American imagination a stereotyped image of all Muslims as angry and dangerous conspirators, fixed on spreading hatred, destruction and murder.* We often hear the claim that "Sure, I guess not all Muslims are terrorists, but how come the good ones never speak out? It seems as if they're all willing to support terrorism, even if they don't participate."

Curious about this, I recently typed in the phrase "Muslims Against Terrorism" on the YouTube website, and it brought up 5,470 videos. Then I went to the Google site and typed in the phrase "Muslims who speak out against Violence", and it turned up 24,400,000 results.

The only reason some people have never heard Muslims object to terror and violence is that they do not listen and they have chosen not to look.

Most Americans do not know very much about Islam other than the sensationalism we hear about on the news, so

---

* For that matter, and even acknowledging the obvious liberal (or neoliberal) bias in much of the news media, it is telling that in the wake of a rare apology by Fox News (after they broadcast the extremist and overtly false anti-Muslim views and accusations of a contributor), the Pulitzer Prize-winning columnist Leonard Pitts Jr. of the *Miami Herald* could only lament that in America, "it has come to seem normal that a major news organization functions as the propaganda arm of an extremist political ideology, that it spews a constant stream of racism, sexism, homophobia, Islamophobia, paranoia and manufactured outrage, and that it does so with brazen disregard for what is factual, what is right, what is fair, what is balanced —virtues that are supposed to be the *sine qua non* of anything calling itself a newsroom." (Leonard Pitts Jr., "Fox Faux News Forces Rare Apology," Miami Herald, January 24, 2015)

it would be worthwhile to take a look at some of what the Qur'an actually says.

For instance, does the Qur'an sanction forced conversions? In fact, all Islamic jurists, without exception, have held throughout history that any attempt at coercing a non-believer to accept the faith of Islam is a grievous sin. This quote from Chapter 2 could not be any clearer: "There is no compulsion in matters of religion."[93]

The Qur'an does allow Muslims to fight against people who have attacked them or oppressed them (and by the way, the battles that are described in the Qur'an are not being fought against Christians or Jews: they are defensive wars against *other Arabs* who resented Mohammad because they did not want to give up their various idols and did not like the way his anti-idolatry preaching was annoying the pilgrims who came to Mecca each year and made them rich). So Muslims were allowed to fight back when attacked, but in Chapter 60 it says, "God does not forbid you to be kind and equitable to those who have neither fought against your faith nor driven you out of your homes. In fact, God loves the equitable."

And as far as Jews and Christians and other peoples *are* concerned, in Chapter 49 God says, "We have ...made you into nations and tribes, so that you may come to know each other and to honor each other, not so that you should despise each other."

Does the Qur'an say "Kill them wherever you encounter them"? Yes, it does. But contrary to the wild imaginings of frightened westerners, and the lunatic fringe of Islamic terrorists, this verse is not condoning slaughter. It was said in the context of *one particular battle*. The immediately preceding verse says, "And fight in God's cause against those who wage war against you, but do not commit aggression – for verily, God does not love aggressors." The immediately following verse says, "If they desist, God is much forgiving: If they desist, then all hostilities shall cease." In fact, every Qur'anic reference to fighting in a war is qualified by some moral condition of restraint: Muslims are commanded not to commit injustice, they are not to use violence disproportionate to that which threatens them, and they are not to use violence at all when credible avenues to peace are available.

Of course, God also says, "Terror and dread shall fall upon them; by the greatness of your arm shall they be still as stone." But he said that in the Book of *Exodus*. And then there is this quote: "At that time we took all his cities and completely destroyed them – men, women and children. We left no survivors." That was Moses in *Deuteronomy*.

Is the *New* Testament free of such language? In *Luke*, Jesus says, "I have come to cast fire upon the Earth… Do you suppose that I came to grant peace on Earth? I tell you No, but rather division." Later he adds, "Whoever has no sword is to sell his coat and buy one."

What about stoning women who commit adultery? Actually, no such punishment is ever mentioned in the Qur'an. In fact, the Qur'an says nothing at all on the subject. There are a few times when stoning is mentioned in the text, but each time it is a threat being made by *non*-Muslims about what they might do to Muslims. Never does Allah or Mohammad advocate such a thing.

To be completely transparent, there is an Islamic story, *not* in the Qur'an, where an adulteress comes to Mohammad asking to be punished, wishing to be purified so she will not have to "spend eternity in Hell". At first, the Prophet did not know what to do, since there had been no divine revelation on the subject. So he went to see some Jewish scholars he was friends with to see if they had any suggestions, and he found out that the Torah talks about stoning adulterers. The Jews tried to hide this from him – probably because the injunction had *never* been taken literally and was never enforced, and they did not want him to! But the story says he did follow the written Jewish law, had her stoned, and because no divine Revelation ever came to him in which God objected (or mentioned it at all), the punishment was later absorbed because of this silence into Islamic law. The story may or may not have been fabricated or embellished. In any case, it is a unique story in that the victim *asked* to be punished, and nothing in the Qur'an itself ever permits such barbarity.

As to the famous Gospel story about Jesus preventing a mob from stoning an alleged adulteress, most biblical scholars agree that Jesus' act of mercy was not out of keeping with the religious practice of the times. Other Rabbis would not have enforced the *Leviticus* code for stoning an adulteress; none would have said, "go on, stone her." Jesus' stance was well within his Jewish tradition.

It is certainly long past time for Muslim political authorities to take the same stance.

Some people are astonished that Islam would sanction a suicide bomber. In fact, suicide is forbidden in Islam. It was not Allah*, it was not Mohammad – *it was Ayatollah Khomeini* who said, "The purest joy in Islam is to kill or be killed for Allah." Nowhere in the Qur'an is there any justification for suicide or any indiscriminate slaughter.

Here is my favorite quote from the Qur'an, from Chapter 5: "If God had so willed, He could surely have made you all one single community. But He willed it otherwise in order to test you by what he has vouchsafed to [each different tradition]. Vie, then, with one another in doing good works!"

Lastly, here is an example of a Qur'anic verse that has often been used to justify violence and war, that extremists have used to brainwash their young followers, and fear-mongers have used to support their stereotypes. "Unto all hath Allah promised good: But those who strive and fight hath he distinguished above those who sit at home."

But consider: You can "strive and fight" within your own self, against your own negativity, your own moral weakness, your own cynicism and fear. You can "strive and fight"

---

* The word 'Allah' means 'God'. Allah is not some 'different' God from the one that Christians and Jews worship. The Muslim phrase that is often translated as "There is no God but Allah…" is more appropriately translated as "There is no God but God…." It is a statement proclaiming a belief in monotheism, as taught by Abraham, Isaac, Jacob, Ishmael, Jesus, and Mohammad. We are all children of the same God.

against emotional chaos, apathy, complacency and ignorance. I doubt many people of faith – *any* faith – would be shocked to hear that God has a special regard for those who "strive and fight" in this way.

Why do I think this interpretation of the story is relevant? Because on the ride home from their final battle, Mohammad said to his Companions, "We have returned from the Lesser Holy War to the Greater Holy War." When one of them asked him, "What is the Greater Holy War?" he replied, "The war within the soul."

That is the actual meaning of the word *jihad*.

~

I hope this helps people see that Islam is not a religion of violence, any more than Judaism or Christianity are, and that the sacred scriptures of Islam, like any other holy book, must be read in historical context, the words must be read within their own grammatical and linguistic context, and the stories need to be pondered, contemplated and *interpreted* for their inner spiritual meaning.

Unfortunately, that cannot be the end of this discussion of Islam. We cannot take this information in and ignore contemporary reality. We cannot disregard the constant threat of terror that we are living with.

But the religion of Islam, *per se*, is not the cause of war or terror. It is never religion itself that causes such misery. It is people who *manipulate* religion. The religion of Islam is not threatening anyone's way of life. But the *politicization* of Islam clearly is. And it is threatening Muslims as much as or more than anyone else.

Historically, extremist groups have always been marginalized and rejected by mainstream Islam as heretical aberrations.[94] But now a major change has occurred. The magnificent Islamic civilization of the Middle Ages has crumbled, and traditional institutions that once sustained and promulgated Islamic theology – and marginalized extremism – have been taken over by state institutions.

A thousand years ago, at the height of Islamic power, the tradition called *Ijtihad* – the spirit of discussion, debate and dissent – flourished, and was presided over by a class of religious scholars, independent of the political system, called jurists. From the 8th to the 12th century, some 135 schools of Islamic interpretation existed, as well as 70 great libraries. Divergent opinions and schools of thought were not only tolerated, they were celebrated. There was discrimination, and it was hardly an interfaith utopia, but historical evidence indicates that Jews living under Islam experienced much less persecution than the Jews living in European Christendom. Science and art thrived, and Islamic civilization laid the groundwork for the Renaissance.

But in the centuries since, following the Crusades and the later invasions by Genghis Khan and his successors, as well as the inevitable internal political disputes and intrigues as opponents battled each other for power in a vast empire, the world has seen the demise of this high civilization, the stifling of *Ijtihad*, the closing of schools, the repression of critical independent thought, as the duty of the jurists has been co-opted by nationalistic politicians – technocrats serving as self-appointed arbiters of faith – who limit debate and interpretation, rather than expanding it, all to prop up their cultural and political goals and maintain the *status quo*. Now Muslims in these countries are silenced by relentless propaganda warning them that unity and strength demand conformity, debate only causes division, and division is synonymous with criminal heresy.

Many people in this situation have been beaten into emotional submission, which is what the powers-that-be want. No doubt others continue to have questions and diverse opinions, but dare not speak for fear of retaliation.

Fanatic groups, like al-Qaeda, ISIS, and the Taliban (originally supported by the West as allies in our battle with the Soviet Union in Afghanistan, but now virulently anti-American after seeing so much carnage), are still intellectually and sociologically marginalized in Islam. But their highly visible acts of violence command the public stage. Nonetheless, I believe these fanatics will not achieve their ambition to remake the religious landscape of the

Islamic world in their narrow image. There are too many rival traditions. The desire for freedom is too strong. And as Walter Russell Mead has noted, against the drive for a more closed and narrow view of Islam "the Internet is making the great works of Islamic scholarship available to tens of millions of Muslims, including women, who can and will be free to draw their own conclusions about what their faith means and how it should be lived. Theological diversity within Islam seems bound to increase."[95]

In the meantime, it is important to understand that the supremacist thinking of Muslim extremists is grounded in culture, politics and nationalism – not religion. A culture of misguided 'Honor' has eroded the religion of Islam. 'Honor' is an Arab cultural tradition that stresses the family or tribe over the individual. This custom is not Islamic – and for that matter, 80% of the world's Muslims are not Arabic! – but many Muslims, like many fundamentalist Christian Americans, confuse politics with religion.

Under the Arab code of honor, Muslims are taught to abdicate their individuality and accept their fate as property of their family or tribe. It is this cultural tradition that silences reasoning and dissent, and at its worst leads to tragedy when a family feels *shame* and imagines they are compelled to murder their own children. Honor killings, genital mutilation, forced marriages of children, imprisoning innocent women because they have been attacked by rapists, and other disgraceful atrocities, have been defended for far too long in the Arab world under the guise of tradition, despite what the Qur'an (and common decency) teach, and overlooked for far too long in the Western world under the guise of respecting other cultures.

To be fair, however: In recent times a number of current and former members of the U.S. military have told a district court that they were raped, assaulted or harassed during their service; that reports of sexual abuse of American servicewomen are routinely ignored; and that victims are retaliated against. The Defense Department recently estimated that 19,000 assaults occurred within the military in 2010, with 85 percent going unreported.[96] Women who did report them have been demoted, jailed, told they are lying, told they are crazy, and discharged from service with loss of benefits. Recent Pentagon studies suggest that little has changed. Violent sexist behavior, followed disgracefully by either denial or by blaming and punishing the victim, is by no means the exclusive province of Arab societies.

Meanwhile, in Palestine, Hamas relentlessly preaches to their subjects that the Middle East crisis is solely the fault of diabolical, subhuman Jews, who must therefore be killed. The total annihilation of Israel and its people is their all-consuming goal. They reject any offers of peace *because peace is not what they want*. And land is not what they want. Previous offers of "land for peace", previous offers of cease-fires, have brought no respite from attacks. Terrorist regimes see peace overtures as weakness, and they prey on weakness.

But peace is what mothers and fathers and families want, it is what good decent people – *whether Muslim, Christian or Jew* – who simply wish to live their lives and raise their children, want. I suspect the only way it will finally be achieved – and it *will* finally be achieved – is when people rise up and rid themselves of rulers and fanatics who cavalierly sacrifice them on an altar of their political egos and their pathological hatred, who proudly admit they would rather see their own people suffer for a hundred years, than live in peace and prosperity with neighbors. From 2004 to 2008, 85% of al-Qaeda's victims were Muslims: it doesn't take the US or Israel to carry out barbarity against innocent Muslim families.

The vast majority of Muslim people want peace. But in many ways, as history has taught us too many times, this is unfortunately irrelevant: just as it was irrelevant that most Germans weren't Nazis, or most Russians weren't Stalinists. *The terrorists must be stopped.* Like Arjuna, we have no choice. But it must be done without indulging in hatred.

Which is not to say that Israel is innocent. Such people are still few and far between, but there are extremists in Israel who openly talk about expulsion and ethnic cleansing of Israeli Arabs. There have been examples of viciousness and lawlessness in attacks on innocent Muslims. Peaceful non-political Palestinians are still not able to control their money and resources, move about freely, or in many cases be assured of clean water. Although Hamas is clearly responsible for endlessly provoking Israel (with little or no concern for the safety and well-being of their own people) by launching thousands upon thousands of rockets against Israeli cities through the years, a case can certainly be made that Israel, with its far stronger military, has oftentimes responded in a disproportionate way – and that even with the efforts they make to protect civilian life, far too many men, women and children have been wounded or killed, thus punishing innocent Palestinians and driving their loved ones toward the extremist camp.

This does not mean that Israel should not return fire. If Hamas can attack Israel without paying a price they might never stop doing it – responding to attacks is a necessary expedient. But it will never end the conflict, it will never bring security or peace. It merely perpetuates an endless cycle of adolescent vengefulness – Hamas fires rockets, Israel bombs and destroys them, Hamas builds new ones, and bitter Palestinian survivors fire them. Like the Capulets and the Montagues, like the Hatfields and the McCoys, the situation is getting to a point where the cycle of violence becomes an end unto itself and no one even remembers or cares why they keep doing it.

As is true for all terrorist regimes, Hamas' greatest ally is despair. They grow stronger and more encouraged as Palestinians lose hope of ever being allowed to live in peace, with dignity and self-respect, with happiness and prosperity. Nothing would weaken Hamas more than encouraging Palestinians to have hope in the future, to have faith that nonviolence, cooperation and friendship *are* possible. There are plenty of military and political steps which are going to have to be worked out and concluded, but if the Israelis ever want to stop spending all their energy destroying rockets, they are going to have to *stop destroying hope*.

It is now critical and only *just* that Israel listen far more compassionately to the viewpoint of Palestinians – after all, how would any of us respond if we were suddenly told by a group of outsiders that our homes were no longer ours, the land where our families had lived for generations and where we had raised our children was about to be taken away, that the state where we live was henceforward the new sovereign homeland of the Native American peoples, who claim it as their divine inheritance, in recompense for all the terror and slaughter of the past, just as the Nazis had terrorized and slaughtered European Jews? Might this not cause years upon years of anger, hostility, and violence?

The two sides have to keep talking, they have to keep negotiating. But the only realistic path to peace is through an *unequivocal rejection of hatred, cruelty, and terror,* by all decent people, on all sides, who choose love over hate and life over death.

And I am hopeful, because sooner or later wisdom and decency always win out.

There is much that has to be done to bring about peace, but arguably the most important requirement is that *each one of us* becomes a living example of peace, justice, compassion and love. This is always an option. Consider this: We are all familiar with the stories of 'righteous gentiles', the many noble and courageous Christians who risked, and sometimes lost, their lives, helping to save European Jews from the Holocaust. But here is a story you might not know: During the Nazi occupation, entire Muslim villages in the small country of Albania sheltered Jews. During the previous years, as German Jews scrambled to get visas to escape the coming nightmare, country after country turned them away. Even the United States had a 'quota' for Jews, and turned away many thousands. But the Albanian Embassy granted visas without question. You see, there was no concept of 'stranger' in Albanian culture. For the Muslims of Albania, a 'Foreigner' was a 'Guest', and they were treated with the same hospitality as the three angels who visited Abraham.

All of us, regardless of our race, religion, nationality, gender, or sexual orientation, are part of the Oneness of creation. All of life, as Martin Luther King taught us, is interrelated. "We are all caught in an inescapable network of mutuality, tied into a single garment of destiny.... This is the way our universe is structured.... We aren't going to have peace on Earth until we recognize this basic fact of the interrelated structure of all reality."[97]

~

I will conclude this chapter on tolerance with a story about the famous Trappist monk, Thomas Merton. One day, on a busy street in Louisville, Kentucky, Merton found himself surrounded by people of different religions, different races, and different genders. He suddenly experienced what he called a "radical sensation of inclusion." He later said about this moment:

> I was suddenly overwhelmed with the realization that I loved all those people, that they were mine and I theirs, that we could not be alien to one another even though we were total strangers.

> It was like waking from a dream of separateness, of spurious self-isolation in a special world, the world of renunciation and supposed holiness. ... The sense of liberation from this illusion of difference was such a joy to me and such a relief, that I almost laughed out loud.

> It is a glorious destiny to be a member of the human race.[98]

CHAPTER EIGHT

THE STEWARDS OF THE EARTH

We have been promised that through a combination of enlightened commercial policies and advances in science and technology we will eventually usher in a wonderful future. But in fact, we are causing immense ruin to the world around us. This disconnect persists in part, as noted previously, because while politics, economics and technology have an important place in our lives, they are only valuable and effective when they are ruled by men and women of conscience. But when conscience succumbs to meaninglessness, as we witness all too often, values are cheapened and become short-sighted, and they are re-concocted anew each day by fashion, whim, and our demands for entertainment and comfort. Politics, economics and technology then become the rulers, and we become their slaves. The only way these things can be a positive force for good is if we become conscious, responsible, honest and loving, use our intelligence, and refuse to ignore or make excuses for harsh realities.

Since the time of the first European explorers, there has been a basic and "disturbing commitment," in the words of Thomas Berry, "to conquer this continent and reduce it to human use."[99] This "exaltation of the human" coupled with the "subjugation of the natural" has been so excessive, Berry notes, that we are today forced to look for a fresh understanding of "how the human community and the living forms of Earth might now become a life-giving presence to each other," rather than perpetuating the unconscious, life-destroying, violent competition between humanity and the world, that is grounded in the misguided and maladaptive 'onlooker' viewpoint of 19th-century science and the hollow presumption that accumulating wealth takes precedence over all other human obligations and aspirations.

This ought to be a goal of education, but our educational system, from pre-school to university, has routinely been collusive with the goals of exploitation. Only in the fields of art, music, literature, and occasionally in philosophy and some of the biological sciences, has the world outside our petty human cravings been given any actual substantive respect and attention, and for the most part these are precisely the fields that are considered 'soft', nonessential, and expendable in today's education marketplace.

The great achievements of the European settlers in the Americas – establishing a place where freedom could flourish, where people could worship or not worship as they please, where all individuals (not just the rich or "high born") would have the same rights and opportunities, where governance would be determined *by* the governed and not merely imposed *on* the governed – have been flawed from the very start by the dual corruptions of murdering and enslaving people, and plundering the land. The great achievements of science, technology, and economic insight that have helped bring about much relief from poverty, hunger, and sickness, have been accompanied by the thoughtless devastation of that very environment that is necessary for the perpetuation and prospering of life. Most of those who helped bring about our current way of life saw only the bright side of their achievements, uninterested in their ethical failures, unconcerned with the consequences of their political and commercial obsessions that have caused so much damage to the planet – which has routinely been treated as an "it" that exists only to slavishly serve us. "We behave in the family of Nature," wrote A. R. Orage nearly a century ago, "like self-indulgent children whose only object is to enjoy ourselves. If you will only ponder seriously for half an hour on the way we exploit natural resources, land, forests, and animals, for the gratification of abnormal desires, you cannot help but be appalled."[100]

We all have learned the lesson, even when we forget to follow it, that other people are not in existence merely for us to use them. But we are still quite some distance from

166

grasping the parallel truth that other living things, and the Earth itself, are also not in existence merely so that we can use them. It will take a great deal of emotional and intellectual maturity to realize this, and we will have to move beyond "our exquisitely stupid cleverness." But it is time to grow up.

Those who continue to deny ecological devastation or to belittle its effects, rely on the evidence of past ages in which the demands that mankind placed on the natural environment have always been manageable. They therefore scoff at any suggestion that they might not *continue* to be manageable indefinitely into the future. Neither logic nor physical evidence can support this presumption, which often coincides ironically with feelings of great pride in the extraordinary technological and industrial inventiveness of recent years – which is precisely what is creating so many never-before-heard-of burdens on planetary biochemistry, climatology, geology and ecology. Loss of topsoil, extinction of species, wholesale destruction of rainforests, rapid forced evolution of virulent pathogens, overburdened systems of waste disposal, are just a few of the effects that our lack of consciousness, wisdom, and conscience are bringing about at a rapid pace – a pace that our band-aid mentality (i.e., waiting until something that was probably preventable has gone horribly and dangerously wrong and then indignantly demanding a 'cure') will not be able to keep up with indefinitely. Nonetheless, this way of thinking is what supporters of fracking, pipelines, and nuclear energy, continue to rely on while insisting that some possible economic advantages are all that really matter.

Berry believed that the deepest underlying cause of our present circumstances "is found in a mode of consciousness that has established a radical discontinuity between the human and other modes of being and the bestowal of all rights on the humans."[101] This means that plant-life and animal-life, as well as rivers, oceans, and mountains, only have a right to exist if we, in our deluded self-importance, decide that we have a use for them. All our political,

167

business, educational, cultural, and religious establishments are deeply "committed consciously or unconsciously to a radical discontinuity between the human and the nonhuman."[102] (The numbers of religious people who claim to be devout believers and followers of God, who nonetheless demonstrate precious little love or respect for what that God has supposedly created – and what He, according to the Bible, says is 'Good" – is endlessly baffling to me.)

Where does this line of thinking come from? Why do many of us so quickly and automatically assume that our interests always come first, and if something is profitable and expedient we do not need to consider anything else? An answer is found in the combination of childish conceit endorsed by religious misunderstanding.

In *Genesis*, we are told that humans are to have dominion here on Earth. This morning, as I was driving cautiously into town because of all the snow that was falling on the road, the weatherman on the radio informed me that there would be no snow today. Somehow, evidently, nature has not heard that we have dominion over her and she is supposed to do what we say. All those pesky tornadoes, shark attacks, and circus animal rampages, also seem to suggest that for some reason or other nature is not obeying us as she should.

Or perhaps 'dominion' means something else. Perhaps it does not give us the right to behave however we wish, or to ruin, enslave, or kill whatever we wish. Perhaps it does not grant us the right to plunder and disrupt, flaunting our power, our wastefulness, our selfishness and disdain. Perhaps it means to tend, care for, and cultivate. Perhaps having dominion means we are expected to be *enlightened* rulers who are charged with the *responsibility* of *protecting* and *serving* our domain like adults, and are not granted *carte blanche* to be bludgeoning egotistical tyrants.

This sort of tyranny can only exist if we see ourselves as separate from the nature we are tyrannizing. What is needed now is to recover that ancient sense of oneness and interrelatedness with the world, without having to give up the equally important modern sense of individual selfhood and personal freedom. But can material separateness be reconciled with spiritual wholeness, or are we forced to make an absolute and immutable choice between them?

The solution to this dilemma lies in a deepened understanding of levels of Being.

According to the classic scientific model of the world, the only level of reality that exists is the one we can see, touch, measure and weigh. This implicit assumption, that everything in existence can be observed by our senses and studied in a laboratory, has provided the necessary theoretical foundation for scientific progress.

But spiritual traditions have always agreed with Plato, Buddha, Christ, the world's Shamans and others, that there is *more than one* level of reality – at the very least, there is an 'Above' and a 'Below'. The words 'Above' and 'Below', unfortunately, are inadequate and misleading. The levels we are talking about do not refer to different *locations*. They refer to different *states of Being*.

The material level of reality, the level that *can* be observed, touched, and measured, is the domain of science, and *religion has no business arguing with its magnificent discoveries.* At the same time, *science has no business pretending that it understands the human soul* – once we speak of *invisible subjective experience* we are completely outside the realm of science, for we are no longer speaking of material phenomena. A thought, a feeling, a wish, cannot be taken out of the soul and placed inside a test tube to be observed and experimented upon. (The objection that we may eventually *be* able to take the elements inside the brain that are involved with a thought or feeling, and study their make-up and their activity in an experimental setting, is spurious. We certainly will be able to learn a great deal of interesting and extremely useful information from an analysis of these molecules and their actions. But the movements-of-molecules during the experiencing-of-a-thought are not the thought *itself.* They are just synchronous movements of material *substances* during an immaterial cognitive *experience*, just as the *children playing tag* are not identical with the inner *experience of seeing* them.)

Science has its rightful place in our lives, and spirituality has its rightful place as well. They perform their work on two different, yet complementary, levels (and thus are 'two' and 'one' simultaneously – two superimposed levels comprising one continuum), and as Plato realized long ago, there is *no conflict between them.*

Einstein understood this too. In his book, *Out of My Later Years,* he wrote:

> All religions, arts and sciences are branches of the same tree. All these aspirations are directed toward ennobling man's life, lifting it from the sphere of mere physical existence and leading the individual towards freedom.... Both churches and universities – so far as they live up to their true function – serve the ennoblement of the individual.[103]

As mentioned in Chapter One, the purpose of science is to unravel mysteries within the physical world. It is not the purpose (or capability) of science to discover a sacred meaning *behind* the physical world or to arrogantly pretend to 'prove' that no such meaning exists. The purpose of religion is not to explain material phenomena or to tell us what 'really' happened in history. The purpose of religion is to help us perfect our inner souls and discover life's meaning for ourselves. We can appreciate *both* of these complementary levels of reality precisely because we, too, are a unique and unified combination of matter and spirit! As human beings it is our obligation to strive for an understanding of the mechanisms of the physical world while simultaneously striving to consciously experience the divine.

Because both of these levels of Being exist simultaneously, we *can* be a separate, rational, independent 'self', *and* be immersed in the sacred Oneness of existence, simultaneously. But when we plunder the Earth, we have implicitly accepted the viewpoint that only one level of reality exists, the material level regarding which our minds are merely disconnected 'onlookers', and Earth only exists 'out there'. The deepest wounds to the Earth, and the deepest wounds to the human soul, have been caused by this lack of appreciation of levels – with the concomitant loss of a participatory experience of unity, and the glorification of the mundane. And thus, we find ourselves at odds with the planet that sustains us. We research her and exploit her as an object to be studied, controlled and used, for the Earth has become for us an unrelated 'it', rather than a related 'thou'.

The result is that we then no longer experience a universe filled with beauty, radiance, and life. We experience it only as some-*thing* that is outside us, mechanical, pedestrian, hopefully of use to us, for we believe that we are the center of everything and everything 'else' revolves around us.

But this way of thinking, fortunately, is ultimately doomed. In his book *Global Awakening*[104], Michael Schacker points out its correlation with the previous and parallel belief that the *Earth* was the center of the universe – a belief that caused not only great misunderstandings in science, but also great misunderstandings in human psychology, religion, and politics. When this idea was finally overthrown in the wake of the Copernican Revolution, the new understanding of our place in the universe eventually led to the end of feudalism, the divine right of kings, and much religious oppression, all of which ultimately opened the door for the appearance of modern western democracy. Now, he points out, a *new* revolution has occurred in our scientific understanding, the revolution of Relativity and Quantum Theory. We are stuck where we are because of the usual cultural lag in grasping its significance universally, but this revolution, like its predecessor, has completely altered the very foundations of scientific thinking and the once-solid underpinnings of much contemporary human wisdom. As a result, the next historical phase, which is already unfolding, includes the recognition that *we* are not the center of the universe either, everything does *not* revolve around us: the scientific revelations of the early 20th century have made it clear that we are not just separate individuals, but are simultaneously immersed in nature as part of an organic *whole*. Once this is fully accepted, which is inevitable, Schacker predicts that we will again see great changes in human psychology, spirituality, and politics, including an end to the sociopathic arrogance and greed that have caused so much ecological devastation, and so much violence, hatred, and war.

In fact, he suggests that the current conservative backlash in America and elsewhere (including the rise of religious fundamentalism in response to perceived threats to religious beliefs, and the rise of political conservatism in response to perceived threats to political and patriotic beliefs), much like the fundamentalist and conservative backlash that occurred in the 1730's not long after the revelations of Copernicus, is a necessary and normal step along the historical pattern that always underlies large-scale growth and change – but happily, notwithstanding the recent election of Trump, *this backlash is now in its last gasps*.

Dylan may have spoken a bit too soon and the 1960's may have been a little premature, but the times they are a'changing.

~

Contrary to our long history of confusing the noble concept of 'dominion' with the vulgar concept of 'domination', the biblical tradition clearly maintains that God is concerned with *all* life on Earth, and human beings have an obligation to *care* for our planetary home and all the planet's creatures.* In *Exodus*, God determines that Moses is ready to fulfill his task when He sees that Moses is merciful toward animals. According to the prophet Hosea, God says "I will make a covenant on behalf of Israel with the wild beasts, the birds of the air, and the things that creep on the

---

* I have discussed elsewhere the knotty issue of the ancient Israelite cult of animal sacrifice. (See *Symbols, Meaning, and the Sacred Quest: Spiritual Awakening in Jewish, Christian and Islamic Stories.*)

earth ... so that all living creatures may lie down without fear." (Hos 2:18). Proverbs states simply, "A righteous man cares for his beast." (12:10) The Jewish physician and scholar, Moses Maimonides, would later say, "It should not be believed that all beings exist for the sake of the existence of man. On the contrary, all the other beings too have been intended for their own sakes and not for the sake of anything else."

The eastern religions of Buddhism, Hinduism and Jainism all urge compassion for animals in recognition of the Oneness of life. *Ahimsa,* the central ethical doctrine of these traditions, is the principle of not causing pain or harm to others. Buddha commanded his followers not to kill animals, for acts of violence toward living things, in order to get what we want, is a horrific cause of attachment and only binds us ever more tightly to our suffering.* Buddhism seeks release from suffering.

Mohammad taught his followers that "Whoever is merciful even to a sparrow, God will be merciful to him on the Day of Judgment." He also said that "A good deed done to an animal is as meritorious as a good deed done to a human being, while an act of cruelty to an animal is as bad as an act of cruelty to a human being."[105]

In Christianity, Pope John Paul II wrote that "Creation was given and entrusted to humankind as a duty", i.e., not a personal plaything, and God says of all creation "It is good that you exist."[106] St. Francis understood well that "If you have men who will exclude any of God's creatures from the shelter of compassion and pity, you will have men who will deal likewise with their fellow men."

---

* The Buddhist concern with suffering does not mean that life is a terrible and depressing experience, with nothing but ugliness and pain. There is much beauty and joy in life: love, children, nature, music, art, sexuality, the life of the mind, the life of the body, the life of the emotions, the life of the spirit. All of this is wonderful. It is also fleeting. And when we *cling* to it, when we remain *attached* to it, when we identify with it and make it our God (the Bible calls this *idol worship*), we sooner or later discover the truth of the Buddha's warning about suffering.

It is by no means just the voices of religion that keep trying to get this message through to us. The well-known atheist, Christopher Hitchens, wrote, "when I read of the possible annihilation of the elephant or the whale, or the pouring of oven cleaner or cosmetics into the eyes of live kittens, or the close confinement of pigs and calves in lightless pens, I feel myself confronted by human stupidity, which I recognize as an enemy."[107] Cruelty and stupidity, he correctly points out, are often close companions.

Among scientists, Einstein spoke of "widening our circle of compassion to embrace all living creatures and the whole of nature in its beauty,"[108] and he warned that "any society which does not insist upon respect for all life must necessarily decay."[109] Charles Darwin thought that "The love for all living creatures [is] the most noble attribute of man."[110] The American inventor, Thomas Edison, believed that "Non-violence leads to the highest ethics, which is the goal of all evolution. Until we stop harming all other living beings, we are still savages."[111] Pythagoras knew that "as long as men massacre animals, they will kill each other." Rachel Carsen added, "It is a wholesome and necessary thing for us to turn again to the earth and in the contemplation of her beauties to know of wonder and humility."[112]

In his book *The Basis of Morality,* Schopenhauer wrote that "The assumption that animals are without rights and the illusion that our treatment of them has no moral significance is a positively outrageous example of Western crudity and barbarity. Universal compassion is the only guarantee of morality."[113] Even earlier, Immanuel Kant became one of many thoughtful people who have always maintained that "We can judge the heart of a man by his treatment of animals."[114]

"Anyone who has accustomed himself to regard the life of any living creature as worthless," said Albert Schweitzer, "is in danger of arriving also at the idea of worthless human lives."[115] This principle was perhaps stated most vividly in a quote that is often attributed to Theodor W. Adorno, though he never actually said it. It's too bad. Whoever may have said it, it has a definite ring of truth: "Auschwitz begins wherever someone looks at a slaughterhouse and thinks: they're only animals." (When I see videos of animals screaming in fear in slaughterhouses, or calves jammed into tiny stalls throughout their lives so that our veal will be tender, or a bear jumping into a river to save its cub, or foxes running in maddening circles in their cages where they are being tortured and tormented for their fur that will ripped off their bodies to feed human vanity, I no longer have sympathy for the opinion that calling our treatment of animals a 'holocaust' is an exaggeration and a disservice to WWII holocaust survivors. No, I'm sorry, but I see in these animals decency, love for their families, love for life: these are precisely the qualities that slave owners denied to slaves, that Nazis denied to Jews and their other victims. This denial of the sacredness of all life, this denial of the right of living creatures - human and otherwise – to live their lives, is all of a kind.)

~

The virtually unconscious continuation of the attitude of domination is justified in a number of ways. Primarily, of course, there is the intransigent conceit that we humans are the center of the universe, the pinnacle of creation, and only our desires and concerns are of any real import. There is also the somewhat demented view of a small group of fundamentalists that what we do to the planet really does not matter, since an angry and vindictive God is soon going to destroy it anyway, before saving them and tossing the rest of us into the fire. And there are those who proudly think they are using science and logic when they assure us that animals cannot think, cannot reason, do not have emotions, and therefore do not really care one way or the other what we do to them.

Those who insist on believing the latter are the unknowing heirs of Rene Descartes, the 17th century French philosopher who persuasively argued that the "world" and "I" are totally distinct entities – a radically new idea at the time – and we can objectively study the world without having any connection to it. This was the birth of the "onlooker" perspective that supplied the necessary foundation for classical mechanical science, in which the world became a mere inanimate machine, an unrelated 'it'. One of the more reprehensible consequences of this notion was Descartes' belief that animals are nothing more than organic machines, devoid of language, mind or consciousness, and therefore *humans have no obligation to treat them any differently than we would treat any other machine.* This means we can totally disregard their apparent emotions or any apparent expressions of pain since these are just mechanical impulses. Descartes even advocated dissection of living animals for scientific purposes, since being devoid of mind meant that they could not feel pain, and their screams were merely the irritating noises made by broken machinery.

It does not take very much to refute these arguments, this "brazen lie", in the words of Isaac Bashevis Singer, that we all know "was invented to justify cruelty"[116]. Descartes' theory that animals do not have a mind was mainly based on his observation that they do not speak or communicate. Today we know much more about the various ways that animals *do* in fact communicate. We also know much more about sensations of physical pain and the workings of the nervous system, and we know that we, too, are 'animals', sharing with other life forms the same organs, nerves, cells, and even DNA. In addition, we know that animals have feelings and emotions. In fact, we've known this for quite some time. A century after Descartes, Voltaire would ask the vivisectors, "You discover in it all the same organs of feeling that are in yourself. Answer me, mechanist, has nature arranged all the means of feeling in this animal so that it may not feel?"[117] So the question, according to the famous Utilitarian, Jeremy Bentham, "is not, 'Can they reason?' nor, 'Can they talk?' but 'Can they suffer?'"[118] We know without doubt that the answer to this is affirmative, so the more critical question becomes, "Do we *care?*" And if not, *why* not?

One justification for not caring and for continuing to mistreat animals is the assumption that, even though they have brains and pain fibers, they are not *sentient*. A sentient being has an awareness of itself, and a conscious self-centered interest in avoiding pain and death. Are all animals sentient? We do not know: worms, clams, ants, might be sentient or might not be. Are plants sentient? Possibly to some degree, but here the generally accepted view is that they are not: they are alive, they react to stimuli, but there is no evidence that they have a mind that is aware of itself, or is concerned one way or another with its individual survival. On the other hand, the animals we use for food, for medical experimentation, for the perverse amusement of killing them for 'sport', or to steal their ivory and fur so that we can decorate and glorify our freakish lives, are *clearly* sentient.

If we cannot stop all suffering, we can at least cause as little suffering as possible. That much choice we do have. Even if plants do possess some degree of sentience, it is a disingenuous and specious argument to suggest that the level of blood curdling terror, emotional agony, and physical sensation of pain that is felt by an animal when we destroy its life for our pleasure, is comparable to what is experienced by a vegetable. That's just the sort of nonsense Descartes might have said.

Other justifications include the adamant belief that eating dead animals is an absolute necessity for our health and survival, that the only way to guarantee the safety and efficacy of scientific advances is to test new products and theories on 'less important' living things, that hunting is necessary to keep the deer population under control (or other environmental 'boons'), and various other justifications that similarly do not hold up to scrutiny.

But the real reason for our continuing mistreatment of the environment, of animals, of ourselves, and of each other, is the insidious wish to remain emotionally asleep and comfortable at all costs, to not have to see things as they are, to not be burdened with thinking, or feeling, or with the difficulties and responsibilities of life. We just want to be left in peace so we can forget the suffering of others and our own inner nullity. We would rather not confront the terrible lack of meaning in our lives, or our lack of love and appreciation for ourselves, for each other, for the world. *Eros*, the desire for all that is good, true and beautiful, has fled, and now we just want to be left alone.

How easily, in use Emerson's word, we capitulate! How easily we exchange our freedom and exuberance for comfort and security. How easily we indulge in asinine qualities and head to the stable, rather than feeling the qualities of Gabriel. How easily we forget to say "I Am", to trust our deepest intuitions, to fight against our suggestibility, to think and feel and act *from ourselves,* from that divine spark that we are so ashamed to admit is still there, that place of love and compassion that derives from our unity with all of life and creation.

~

If someone makes a decision to no longer participate in certain old habits and customs, such as eating meat, that no longer feel right to them, the usual accusations of inconsistency almost certainly will arise in a flash: "So, you don't eat steak – but Aha! – your belt is made with leather!" These angry defenders of the status quo and clever rooter-outers-of-hypocrisy, always looking for some weakness to pounce on (rather than being supportive, or at least neutral) will in fact almost certainly uncover various and sundry examples of hypocrisy: and if not, the converse accusation of 'self-righteousness' is always available in its stead. But in the midst of their irritation, all they have really stumbled upon is the simple truism that it is not easy to completely make over one's life and eliminate every possible inconsistency. Nor is it a sane expectation. One does what one can.

Does the recognition that we are unable to completely avoid causing pain in the world, lead inexorably to the conclusion that therefore we might just as well cause intentional pain and not fret about it? When I became a vegan, and quickly recognized how utterly impossible it would be for me to completely live by the standards of compassion that I only *wished* I could attain, I was reminded of a conversation near the end of Albert Camus' book, *The Plague*, between Dr. Rieux and his friend Tarrou (whom I suspect was expressing Camus' own standards). In the midst of so much agony, Tarrou was speaking about human death, but the points he makes about simple decency are, in my opinion, morally applicable to all of life's experiences of pain, suffering, and death:

> For many years I've been ashamed, mortally ashamed, of having been, even with the best intentions, even at many removes, a murderer in my turn. As time went on I merely learned that even those who were better than the rest could not keep themselves nowadays from killing or letting others kill, because such is the logic by which they live; and that we can't stir a finger in this world without the risk of bringing death to somebody. Yes, I've been ashamed ever since; I have realized that we all have plague, and I have lost my peace. And today I am still trying to find it; still trying to understand all those others and not to be the mortal enemy of anyone. I only know that one must do what one can to cease being plague-stricken, and that's the only way we can hope for some peace or, failing that, a decent death. This, and only this, can bring relief to men and, if not save them, at least do them the least harm possible and even, sometimes, a little good. So that is why I resolved to have no truck with anything which, directly or indirectly, for good reasons or bad, brings death to anyone or justifies others' putting him to death.[119]

Tarrou's convictions are also the best argument I know for stopping the irrational, ineffectual, and primitive practice of capital punishment – though this really ought to be a no-brainer given the number of mistakes we know are made and knowing that states without the death penalty have consistently lower homicide rates. Most people also do not realize that death penalty cases can cost taxpayers far more money than life-without-parole cases. But it is the sanctity of life issue that I find the most persuasive, and far more likely to provide an actual effective deterrent: after all, if the government can have a so-called 'good reason' to kill someone, why can't I? Like Tarrou, we need to do all we can to cease being "plague-stricken" – to cease, to the extent possible, being a conscious or unconscious source of pain and death. We need to learn to "have no truck with anything which, directly or indirectly, for good reasons or bad, brings death to anyone or justifies others' putting him to death."

The wish to 'not be the mortal enemy of anyone' also relates to the difficult issue of abortion. If my 'pro-choice' friends wish to be taken seriously on a moral level, I would suggest they be careful not to gloss over the fact that destroying a fetus, at any stage, is destroying life. If my 'pro-life' friends wish to be taken seriously on a moral level, I suggest they stop lecturing others on the evils of abortion while hypocritically discounting the sanctity of life by promoting war, imprisonment, capital punishment, and callous cutbacks in human services.

Both sides can easily agree that life is precious, and it is sad and unfortunate whenever any life must suffer. This is a difficult issue, but there is no reason why it must be such a violently divisive issue. People love to dig in their heels and make childish, ugly insinuations about people who disagree with them, but this could be an ideal opportunity to try out Emerson's suggestion instead: "where debate is earnest, and especially on high questions, the company becomes aware that the thought rises to an equal level in all bosoms.... They all become wiser than they were." I do not believe that anyone holds the hard-hearted opinion that abortion is not a serious matter. But sometimes, choices must be made in our lives even when no choice is a 'good' one, even when there is no perfect solution to a problem. I would like to see far fewer abortions. We all would like to see that. But the way to decrease the number of abortions is *not* to have the government pass, and attempt to enforce, repressive laws. All this does is force women who want an abortion into dark situations where life is even more disrespected and endangered. This is not a political issue, and this is not a Christian issue. It is a universal *moral* issue. It is not the government's business. To decrease the number of abortions, pro-life advocates need to make a case, a moral case (not a sanctimonious *moralistic* case, or a spiteful fundamentalist case), for the genuine beauty and sacredness of life, including the sacredness of sexuality, without disregarding the sacredness of the mother and her right to make moral decisions of her own. They also need to join *with* liberal forces that are attempting to promote education on these issues, and solve the various issues of poverty and despair that are often underlying pieces of the puzzle. And both sides need to persuade corporations and the media to stop relentlessly 'selling' meaningless sex with no responsibility.

~

Another criticism I sometimes hear is the accusation that vegans and other animal rights 'crazies' care more about animals than they do about human beings. Actually, people do not have finite amounts of compassion: feelings of mercy and love are not limited to 'just this much and no more'. Most of the people I know who are concerned with preventing cruelty toward animals, including those who may indeed seem quite obsessive, one-track-minded, and even rather obnoxious about the issue, nonetheless have plenty of room in their hearts for compassion toward children, the elderly, the sick, the poor, the mentally ill, the hurt and abused, as well as their fair share of concern for justice, halting oppression, and ending war.

It is also common to be reminded that one's diet should be respected as one's *personal choice*, and veganism "is just not for them." Here I would only mention that when one's 'choice' has a 'victim', it is no longer 'personal'.

And the victim is not just some particular animal that has suffered and died, though this really ought to be enough to give us pause (to insist that the enjoyment we gain from the taste of a meal is of equivalent value to an entire lifetime cut drastically and violently short, is surely an example of the very worst kind of moral relativism). But there are many *more* victims: the continuous production and consumption of animal foods is one of the leading causes of world hunger and one of the worst threats to the environment.*

It is estimated that 925 million humans around the world suffer from hunger. Every year, starvation kills over 2.5 million children under the age of five. But there is enough food on earth to feed every last man, woman, and child. The problem is that even though there are enough plant-based foods to feed the entire human population, the majority of crops (including those grown in countries where people are starving) are fed to livestock that gets sold to affluent nations. The quandary here is easy to visualize by imagining the amount of food that goes to feed one cow for the one or two years of its life prior to being slaughtered, and then comparing this to the amount of meat that one dead cow generates. This stark comparison shows the staggering degree to which the animal farming industry is illogical and unsustainable. If we stopped intensively breeding farm animals and grew crops to feed humans instead, we could easily feed everyone on the planet with healthy, affordable vegetable foods. (This is not a secret, nor is it a secret that hunger continues because of greed, or that greedy business people will not change their practices as long as *we* do not change *ours*.)

The production of so much animal protein consumes huge amounts of natural resources such as water, fossil fuels, and topsoil, while polluting lakes, streams, and air: consider all the pesticides, fertilizers, fuel and water that are needed

---

* Speaking objectively, the Earth is of course in no danger. It is you and I and all of the life that she sustains that are in peril.

to produce feed for poultry and livestock. Plenty of studies have shown that switching to a plant-based diet is the single most important step that individuals can take to help preserve the environment. According to the Water Education Foundation, it takes 2,464 gallons of water to produce one pound of beef, compared to 25 gallons to produce one pound of wheat. According to the Nature Conservancy, during every second of every day an area of rainforest the size of a football field is cut down in order to raise livestock: that's 55 square feet of tropical rainforest, vital for the world's oxygen supply, per hamburger.

Research also shows that meat production contributes to global warming at a much higher rate than the cultivation of grains and vegetables. A recent study in the U.K. found that meat-eaters had twice the carbon footprint of vegans. Giving up meat would be far more effective on this front than giving up cars.

Of course, none of this would matter if it were true that killing and eating animals is an absolute necessity for human health and survival. So at the risk of droning on a bit, let's take a brief look at some of the facts about this.

One pervasive argument is that "we've always done it", human beings throughout their natural history have eaten meat. This of course proves nothing. First, because the evidence for the assertion itself is questionable and unconvincing, but even more so because one of the main things that makes us 'human' is precisely our potential to rise above our purely physical cravings and use our *minds* to think about morality and to pursue higher values. Just as we are not the helpless victims of our genes, so we are not the helpless victims of our physiological history, even if our ancestors *were* meat-eaters. We are no more compelled to eat like our ancestors than we are to practice cannibalism, rape, slavery, or any other violent tradition that has been an unfortunate part of our human past. The longstanding character of a bad habit or practice does not make it necessary, ethical, or natural.

Nonetheless, it is often said that we are physiologically designed to need animal products in our diet. This is simply false. We can get all the nutrients we need from the plant world. It is true that we are omnivores – which only means we *can* digest and utilize animal products, not that we *must* do so. It is true that we need protein for tissue growth and repair, but there is plenty of protein in plant foods, and surely there have been enough photographs of vegan bodybuilders on the internet to squelch the myth that active people need to eat meat. It is also true that we have canine teeth – but so do gorillas, baboons, some species of deer, and even the hippopotamus, all of whom are vegetarians. (In fact, our innards are virtually identical to other exclusively-vegetarian primates). It is true that we need Vitamin B12, but this can be had from brewer's yeast or nutritional yeast. In fact, it is not really accurate to say that eating animals gives us B12. The B12 in animals is made by bacteria living in their gut, not by the animal itself, and the bacteria in *our* gut does the same thing.

Carnivores are built to run at top speeds for several miles while hunting (humans, by the way, if not given high-powered rifles or other technology, but left to only their natural abilities, are actually rather pathetic hunters). Carnivores have huge stomachs that are designed to eat lots of food once every week or so, when they are able to catch prey. They swallow their food whole, no need for chewing: their stomachs have large amounts of acid for digesting protein and fat, and even dissolving bones, but their saliva has no enzymes for breaking down carbohydrates, so no chewing is necessary. Their jaws and teeth are built for quick ripping and getting the food as fast as possible into the stomach acid. Their intestines are short – meat tends to putrefy rather quickly and needs to be moved along rapidly, and whatever waste is left should leave the body quickly so it doesn't putrefy in the colon and leak toxins into the body. This quick elimination of meat and saturated fat is part of why true carnivores don't suffer from clogged arteries and resultant cardiovascular problems the way humans do.

Plant-eaters, including humans, are built to walk and forage for long periods. Their stomachs are designed to receive food several times each day. Their teeth are different from carnivores and are meant for chewing: saliva contains amylase to begin breaking down carbohydrates, and the jaws are structured for a smaller opening (perfect for plant food) and the ability to move side-to-side (something carnivore jaws cannot do) for grinding up food. Plant-eaters are built to swallow small boluses of well-chewed, partially digested food (the great majority of people who choke to death each year choke on meat). The intestines are long to permit the more complex digestion of plants foods over long periods of time: but this is not a good thing for meat digestion which tends to quickly rot, stink, and exude toxins. Plant-eaters have a much larger appendix, filled with bacteria to break down the cellulose in plants (carnivores don't need these bacteria and have much smaller appendices without these bacteria). Carnivores lap up water, but we plant-eaters use our lips and cheeks for suction to suck water in (possibly because this is much quieter, to avoid being heard by a predator).

I won't go into all the gory details here of the horrible brutality of factory farming and slaughterhouses, mostly because words on a page cannot begin to convey the terror, pain and horror of such practices. I will instead ask readers to go online and, if your stomach can take it, watch a few of the many videos on the subject that can be found on YouTube and elsewhere. Here, I will just note that the cruelty that is routinely inflicted on animals in large factory farms, as well as on small 'free range' farms, includes sexual violation (exploitation of the animal's reproductive system, routine mutilation without anesthetic, forcing excessive pregnancies and then tearing babies away from their mothers in order to steal what is rightfully theirs), the denial of important instinctual behaviors, repulsive conditions of filth, decay, and overcrowding, followed by brutal transport and slaughterhouse conditions. I have heard it claimed that this cannot possibly be true, because if animals were not treated well they would not grow and produce. But farm animals can be horribly mistreated and still grow and produce, just as horribly mistreated humans can still grow fat, be sexually active, and produce milk, eggs, and offspring. Farm animals, like humans, can adapt, and they adapt even more readily with the aid of drugs and breeding techniques. But what they are adapting to is a hellish nightmare, an "eternal Treblinka" in Isaac Bashevis Singer's words.[120]

We are all aware that eating less meat and more vegetables is good for our cardiovascular systems, it can help prevent cancer, and has many other positive benefits for our bodies. But more importantly, I do not believe that torturing and tormenting a living conscious creature, the way we torture and torment animals in the food industry, and then slaughtering it (even 'humanely', or even with all sorts of self-congratulatory rhetoric about thanking it for its 'sacrifice') in order to enjoy how it tastes, is without serious negative consequences for our souls.

Nevertheless, I am in agreement with Christ's point that it is not so much what goes *into* our mouths that defiles us – it's what comes *out*. But if it is possible, and even easy, to eat without killing, without causing bloodshed, pain, and agony, without being the "mortal enemy" of clearly sentient life, why would we do otherwise? And if doing so also improves our health, saves millions of dollars in health care costs, prevents hunger and helps preserve the environment for ourselves and our children, it is surely worth a little bit of struggle against old habits, old comfort levels, and inertia. All of life, all of creation, including ourselves, deserves compassion, respect, and kindness.

~

Of course, kindness and compassion are not the only important virtues. There is also courage, determination, the willingness to sacrifice – all the virtues of the *warrior* side of life. "The military feelings are too deeply grounded," wrote William James, "to abdicate their place among our ideals until better substitutes are offered".[121] Many aspects of militarism cannot be condemned: it preserves ideals of valor, strength, honor, and readiness, while opposing a world of sheep and clerks. The military mind does not deny the horror and expense of war, it simply claims that war is worth it. It sees the alternative as softness, weakness, and a degeneration of the human spirit.

But surely we can find other worthy ways to build the positive character elements that only warfare has built in the past. Surely there can be other forms of challenge and trial, other motives besides hatred, xenophobia, and nationalistic arrogance. James suggested the motives of correcting poverty, racism, and disease. "Great indeed is Fear," he noted, "but it is not, as our military enthusiasts believe and try to make us believe, the only known stimulus for awakening the higher ranges of men's spiritual energies."[122] The Peace Corps, and other volunteer organizations, if properly supported, can help to fill this need, as well as helping people feel invested – a feeling many may have lost.

There are plenty of reasons why we had better find a better way. In his shattering book, *The Fate of the Earth*, Jonathan Schell provided a gruesome description of the consequences of nuclear war – which is just one of the ways, though probably the most dramatic, that we might bring about a final end to life on Earth. Even as he recognizes that it is difficult to read such an account, he also writes that only by descending now through imagination into this hell can we hope to escape entering it in reality later on. To end the poisoning of the planet, our bodies, and our souls, and to prevent a final holocaust, is going to require a deliberate and conscious psychological turn from comfortable forgetting to responsible remembering. This does not mean that we must only remember the repugnant. We must also remember the exquisite joy of being alive.

There are thousands of nuclear warheads on the planet today, adding up to many thousands of megatons of explosive force.* If a one-megaton bomb were to be

---

* According to the Nuclear Notebook, 10,144 nuclear warheads are stockpiled around the globe in 2015. This is marginally good news. At the peak of the Cold War, there were over 60,000 stockpiled nukes.

exploded in the air, the initial radiation would instantly kill people in an area of some 6 square miles: a large bomb detonated over the American heartland would produce an electromagnetic pulse that would damage electrical circuitry throughout the United States, Canada and Mexico, probably bringing all three economies immediately to their knees. The fireball created by a one-megaton bomb would send out a hot thermal pulse capable of causing second-degree burns in an area of 280 square miles: for a large bomb, this area would be over 2,000 square miles. As the fireball burns, it rises into the air, condensing water and raising tons of debris, creating the characteristic mushroom cloud. The dust and water particles mix with the intensely radioactive particles released by the bomb and then fall back to earth with the wind. A one-megaton ground burst could lethally contaminate over a thousand square miles within just a few hours.

All of these effects, plus the massive fires that would ravage vast areas, are the immediate 'local' effects that could be expected from a single nuclear bomb. But if any of these weapons are ever used, it is likely that many will be used. If a few thousand bombs go off in a holocaust (just a fraction of the more than ten thousand that are available), then to the 'local' effects must be added the 'global' effects. Radioactive debris will circulate throughout the atmosphere and contaminate all areas of the planet for months, years, or decades. Some fission products will continue to emit lethal radiation for millions of years. The millions of tons of dust in the air will cause a darkening and cooling of Earth's atmosphere. Much of the ozone layer will be decimated.

> Let us consider...some of the possible ways in which a person in a targeted country might die. He might be incinerated by a fireball or the thermal pulse. He might be lethally irradiated by the initial nuclear radiation. He might be crushed to death or hurled to his death by the blast wave or its debris. He might be lethally irradiated by the local fallout. He might be burned to death in a firestorm. He

might be injured by one or another of these effects and then die of his wounds before he was able to make his way out of the devastated zone in which he found himself. He might die of starvation, because the economy had collapsed and no food was being grown or delivered, or because existing local crops had been killed by radiation, or because the local ecosystem had been ruined, or because the ecosphere of the earth as a whole was collapsing. He might die of cold, for lack of heat and clothing, or of exposure, for lack of shelter. He might be killed by people seeking food or shelter that he had obtained. He might die of an illness spread in an epidemic. He might be killed by exposure to the sun if he stayed outside too long following serious ozone depletion. Or he might be killed by any combination of these perils.[123]

And yet, all such individual deaths would only be "redundant preliminaries, leading up to the extinction of the whole species by a hostile environment." With transportation, communication, and all other parts of the economy destroyed, with the soil, air, and water all contaminated, with disease-breeding dead bodies strewn over the landscape, with survivors screaming and dying painfully, with no medical care, no food supply, and freezing temperatures with no shelter, who among us would even wish to survive?

At issue, then, is not just the wholesale slaughter of millions of people. At issue is any human survival whatsoever. It is not simply a question of killing people. It is a question of *killing the future.* We have become responsible not only for ourselves, not only for our loved ones, not only for our fellow human beings, and not only for the planet and all its life forms. We are responsible for all future generations still unborn. All their possibilities, their rights, their hopes, their joys, and their very lives, are in our hands.

We now decide whether they will ever be permitted to be born.

It is time to stop teaching our children to worship guns and war heroes, and teach them instead to revere the men and women who struggle courageously for justice, peace, and life. Infecting a child's mind with the perverse belief that a psychotic mass-murderer is a figure to be emulated and admired only serves to guarantee our endless, mindless, horrifying enslavement to war and war profiteers. As Stewards of the Earth, let us all make every effort to be conscious, intelligent, and alert. As Victor Frankl noted, "Since Auschwitz we know what man is capable of. And since Hiroshima we know what is at stake."[124]

EPILOGUE

In the end, nothing will change unless *we* change.* If we had never wished to harm one another, there would be no nuclear weapons. If we continue to wish harm upon each other, no political negotiations will protect us. The question each of us must struggle to answer is: why do we feel so much hatred and why are we always so close to violence?

Due to our inner need to feel important rather than empty, we judge, label and divide people into 'classes' and 'categories' that nourish our self-righteous beliefs about good and bad, superior and inferior, right and wrong. Rather than working on our own inner lack of love and compassion, we turn our attention outward and hate our rivals. We try to convert them, we try to talk sense into them, and when all else fails we try to kill them. Racial, religious, misogynistic, nationalistic, and *all* forms of hatred, no matter how subtle, are the deepest roots of violence and war. Rather than pretending to transcend this common human condition, we need to find ways to *transform* it – by transforming ourselves.

The first step, as with any change, is to become conscious of ourselves, and without becoming judgmental or self-disparaging about the negativity we might find, to *stop*

---

* This is not to say that our efforts to improve the external world are pointless. It only means that (as the history of reform movements has shown us over and over again) if we only focus our attention on the external world and neglect to change ourselves, we are merely spinning our wheels and fooling ourselves, and everything of consequence about life on Earth will remain exactly as it was: 'All is vanity,' lamented the wise King Solomon, 'and there is nothing new under the sun.' This is why Gandhi admonished us to "*Be* the change you wish to see in the world" [italics mine]. But it is also true that changing oneself can be a long and arduous process, so I would not have us neglect Marianne Williamson's reminder: "I don't feel there is any spiritual or metaphysical justification for turning our backs on human suffering." Both efforts, the inner and the outer, are simultaneously necessary.

pretending and stop denying. When we clearly see that we have all the same qualities and susceptibilities as everyone else, this by itself can spark an enormous surge of compassion.

As a corollary to this, one invaluable way to initiate this transformation is to make sincere efforts to "put ourselves in other peoples' shoes": to drop our egocentricity and deeply consider the total, internal reality of other living beings. If we could do this, *everything would change.* There could never be another lynching, there could never be another genocide, there could never be another war.

But the most basic and critical step in transforming ourselves is *changing the way we think.* How long will we ignore that inner "gleam of light" that Emerson spoke of? How long will we be "ashamed of that divine idea which each of us represents", dismissing our own inner dreams and ideals with a hopeless sigh, calming ourselves with banal material comforts, and accepting a life of mediocrity and negativity? How long will we remain enslaved to other people's opinions, expectations and demands, letting them tell us what to think, feel, believe, and even buy? Is it true, as has been said, that we are becoming *willing slaves,* and are even growing fond and proud of our slavery? How long will we act small and frightened, hiding from a life of passion, freedom, joy and meaning, denying our role as "collaborators in creation", and merely waiting anxiously for Charon's boat to come and take us away?

Unless our thoughts and attitudes change, unless our minds change, nothing in ourselves or the world will *ever* change, for we will remain forever exactly as we are. This is why Christ's story in the Gospels begins at the Jordan River, where his cousin John is exhorting people to 'repent'. But this is a mistranslation. The Greek word that is translated as 'repentance' is *metanoia,* which actually means *to think in a new and higher way.* All growth in wisdom and character, all spiritual attainment, begins with thinking in a new way. *Metanoia* is the beginning of awakening, the beginning of spiritual maturity.

Later in the story, when Christ says "blessed are the meek," this is again a very misleading mistranslation. The word that has been translated as 'meek' actually signifies a state of consciousness in which our stormy negative thoughts and emotions have been brought under our control. *This* 'meekness' is referring to a dignified, controlled, and reverent surrender to divine guidance through an awakened *Nous*. This is a powerful inner attitude, not a self-degrading, cowardly outer action. Similarly, when he blesses "the poor in spirit", it is *not* because smallness of soul is a good thing. To be 'poor in spirit' means to be *emptied of vain and absurd illusions*, to get out of our own way. This makes room for *Eros* to return – the longing for beauty and truth. Nothing could be more important. The Beatitudes are lessons in how to ascend to higher levels of being.

In contrast, it must be noted that nothing holds us down and binds us to a life of mediocrity and joylessness more completely than our unresolved feelings of indignation, fear, hatred and resentment. A devastating lie that keeps us fearful, worried, disheartened, and endlessly stuck 'in our place' (from which we are always ready to do as we are told), is the oft-repeated insistence that there is not enough prosperity or happiness to go around. But it is only when the world is raped and degraded that 'things run out'. When we treat the world with love, respect and wisdom, we find that this is a world of unbounded possibility, a world of unimaginable abundance. Dwelling on lack and living in fear only breeds unhappiness, greed, stinginess, and destructiveness. We can choose instead to dwell on confidence, on an awareness of the infinite beauty of nature and spirit. We can focus on love, gratitude, the sanctity of life, and what Barack Obama called the audacity of hope. This does not mean we can forego making efforts, or expect to be rewarded without earning a reward, or neglect our responsibilities and just be 'happy'. Hard work, pain, accidents, failure, and overwhelming adversity, are all part of life. But as Victor Frankl noted, even in the most horrible of moments the one imperishable human freedom is the freedom to choose one's attitude in any given set of circumstances. So "follow your bliss," as Joseph Campbell taught, "and the Universe will open doors for you where there were only walls."

~

The way we think about love can also use a good dose of *metanoia*.

Sometimes, what we call 'love' is a function of the body, essentially an experience of chemical attraction – that desperate and dazzling sensation of sexual need and hunger that overtakes us in the presence of certain people, and focuses all our attention on the desire for union with their body and the release of overwhelming physical tension. Purely physical love can be profoundly enjoyable, and as such it is good for the soul and good for a relationship. Our bodies are part of the sacred Oneness of creation, our physical needs are important, and we have a right to enjoy our sexuality. Once the union of bodies and the release of tension have been achieved, however, the 'hunger' disappears, at least temporarily and perhaps even forever. So by *itself*, this kind of love does not sustain a meaningful relationship for very long. Tragically, much of modern culture tries to hypnotize us into believing that this is all the love we should ever expect or aspire to achieve. In consequence, this kind of love is all that some people will ever know.

Most of us, however, still hope for the love that has to do with the heart. This is the kind of love in which we feel a burning need to be utterly fulfilled by the 'beloved' after we have been 'struck by Cupid's Arrow' and we find ourselves hopelessly 'in love'. This is the kind of love that is venerated in much of our literature and art – the exquisite experience of passion, desire, and romance that we all hope we will find and remain immersed in forever. But unless great care is taken, the erotic force of these wonderful emotions will also eventually begin to dissipate, and ultimately even degenerate into something negative. If we turn our attention inward and look honestly and closely at these swirling emotions, we see that they are *passive* emotions. That is, rather than actively loving the beloved, we find a desperate emotional need for the beloved to love *us*. Which is why, after the initial exhilaration of falling 'in love', the situation soon deteriorates into a passive/aggressive demand to *be* loved. This, of course, eventually evokes resentment on the part of the beloved, and we see this happening over and over again in the romantic tragedies of our lives, as couples get together, break up, get together in new pairs, break these up too, maybe finally pair up in marriage, and then spend years tied together in misery and loneliness, or get divorced and continue the same old process all over again. This hopeless floundering between ecstasy and despair is all that most of us will ever know of love.

But there is a third kind of love which has to do with the mind, a *conscious* love that requires us to be *active* – to make the effort to *give* love, regardless of whether any is received in return, even when the beloved happens to be annoying us, even when they are the 'neighbor' that our spiritual traditions often talk about and we do not even know their name, even if they are our 'enemies'. Anyone can feel lovingly toward people when all is going well and people are behaving lovingly toward *us*. When things are *not* going well, when life is difficult – this is when real effort is required to *give* love, and this is when love really means something. When we can honestly wish for the happiness and well-being of another human soul, regardless of their behavior, with no thought to any results for ourselves, this is when love really means something! And it is worth the effort. Emotional love eventually evokes resentment, but sooner or later conscious love evokes conscious love in return.

To love oneself, to love others, to love that which is above us, and to do so *consciously* – this is the whole essence of spirituality. It doesn't matter the tradition. All that matters is that we try to remember and respect that deep longing for all that is beautiful, good and true, that deep longing for personal achievement, passionate relationships, peace on earth, the well-being of others, and union with what is most sacred. Love then fills our lives with joy and meaning.

"Someday," wrote Teilhard de Chardin, "after mastering the winds, the waves, the tides and gravity, we shall harness for God the energies of love, and then, for a second time in the history of the world, man will have discovered fire."[125]

~

Another important step toward transformation is to try to 'remember our death'.

In the late 1980's, while living in New York City and practicing chiropractic, I was asked to join the Board of an organization that was involved with the AIDS epidemic. During the ensuing months, I met a great many people who were HIV positive, a large number of whom had contracted AIDS, and I watched a great many of these new friends die.* It was a heartbreaking time. I remember how hard it was, especially early on, to hear that some young friend had gotten back his or her lab results and had Kaposi's sarcoma or PCP, and was confronting the looming possibility of death. I often had to leave the room on some pretense or other, I found it so hard not to cry or scream.

Then one day, one of my patients told me to stop being so sad. He said that AIDS was the best thing that had ever happened to him. I didn't know what on earth he was talking about, but he explained that once he came to grips with the realization that he (like all of us) was going to die, he stopped

---

* But I hasten to add that *not all* people with HIV or AIDS died. This was one of the things we tried very hard to get people to realize. The relentless media propaganda that "AIDS = DEATH" caused so much fear and terror that the mind, believing what it was told, became a deadly force of negativity and despondency. As a result, many people gave up the fight and spiraled into sickness and death at least partly because they were convinced they were *supposed* to. We tried to counter this with facts – not everyone who contracted AIDS died. So here is a good piece of general advice: don't let the world's negativity, sensationalism and propaganda kill you.

wasting all his time being moody, or cynical, or lazy, or mean, and every moment became a great joy. He said he felt sorry for *me*, and all the people like me who act as if they're going to live forever and can waste all the time they want indulging in negativity.

In her book *On Death and Dying*, Elizabeth Kubler-Ross recognized that only when we truly remember that we are here for just a limited time, and have no way of knowing when our time is up, will we start to live each day to the fullest. She knew that if each of us "would make an all-out effort to contemplate our own death... there could be less destructiveness around us."[126]

In *Journey to Ixtlan*, Carlos Castaneda spoke about this idea in much the same way as my patient. Don Juan was trying to rouse him to see that he must make every moment count passionately, since life only lasts a short while. "There is one simple thing wrong with you – you think you have plenty of time.... This, whatever you're doing now, may be your last act on earth.... There is no power which could guarantee that you are going to live one more minute." Don't waste this final precious moment, don Juan insisted, "on some stupid mood."[127]

So now I try really hard to remember that I am going to die, that I could die in the next moment, that the person I am talking to, or ignoring, or even just thinking about, could die in the next moment – and there will never be another chance to say something kind, helpful, friendly or loving. It's difficult! I fail far more often than I succeed. Someone annoys me, someone cuts me off in traffic, or maybe I'm just tired, and I completely forget. But I *try* to remember what my patient taught me that day. I try to think in a new and better way about the beauty, wonder and fragility of my life, and the miraculous life that is all around me, *because I assure you that nothing in this world is more urgent, more potentially life-changing or more potentially world-changing, than learning to remember one's Death.*

~

Instead of focusing on what's wrong with other people, we need to throw our weight behind our nobler instincts and remember our own highest aspirations. This is the great human quest, the great 'work of art', more important than pyramids, sculptures or cathedrals: can we unite all the conflicting pieces of our confused, fragmented, inner life, to forge a free mind, a free heart, and a free will, reigniting our soul with passion and meaning, and be able to say with Emerson, "I Am"? At the same time, can we bring *Eros* back into our hearts, to help us unite all the broken and fragmented pieces of our *outer* lives, to heal the world with love, to expand our vision beyond ourselves and fully experience our Oneness with all of Creation?

What could possibly be more important, more meaningful, more magnificent, or more worthy of our brief time on Earth, than pursuing this quest?

I am confident that we can and will succeed. In fact, it is inevitable. Somewhere inside us there is a place that is ready to say 'No' to all the hatred, meaninglessness and cruelty, and 'Yes' to all the beauty and nobility of life.

INDEX

200

NOTES AND REFERENCES

1   Sloan, Douglas, *Insight-Imagination: The Emancipation of Thought and the Modern World*, Greenwood Press, Westport, CT, 1983, p.78 (This is an extraordinarily intelligent and insightful book about education, science, and the way we think)

2   Ibid. p. 80

3   Ibid.

4   Larsen, Stephen, *The Fundamentalist Mind,* Quest Books, IL, 2007, p 3

5   Ibid., p. 5

6   Lama Anagarika Govinda, *Creative Meditation and Multi-Dimensional Consciousness,* The Theosophical Publishing House, Wheaton, IL, 1976, p. 217

7   Frankl, Victor, *Man's Search for Meaning,* Washington Square Press (Simon & Schuster), N.Y., 1984 ed., p. 128

8   Ellul, Jacques, *Propaganda*, Random House, New York, 1973, p. 38

9   Berman, Morris, *The Twilight of American Culture,* W.W. Norton, New York, 2006, p. 121

10   Quoted in *Physics and Philosophy: The Revolution in Modern Science,* Werner Heisenberg, Harper and Row, New York, 1958, p. 67

11   Sloan, p. 12 – 13

12   Einstein, Albert, February 12, 1950, in a Letter of Condolence to Robert S. Marcus who had lost his son to polio.

13   Whitehead, Alfred North, *Science and the Modern World,*
     The Macmillan Company, New York, 1925, p. 55

14   Gurdjieff, G.I., quoted in Ouspensky, P.D., *In Search of the
     Miraculous,* Harcourt Brace Jovanovich, FL, 1976, p. 309

15   Peter Sacks, *Standardized Minds,* Perseus Books, New York,
     2000, p. 17

16   Spearman, Charles, *The Abilities of Man,* MacMillan, New
     York, 1927, p. 8

17   Terman, Lewis, *The Measurement of Intelligence,* Houghton
     Mifflin, Boston, 1916, p. 6 - 7

18   Sacks, p. 18

19   All of Emerson's quotations in this chapter are from his
     essay, *Self-Reliance*

20   Williamson, Marianne, *A Return to Love: Reflections on the
     Principles of "A Course in Miracles",* Harper One, San
     Francisco, Reissue Edition 1996, p. 190

21   "Pierre Teilhard de Chardin Quotes." Quotes.net. STANDS4
     LLC, 2015. Web. 3 May 2015.
     http://www.quotes.net/authors/Pierre Teilhard de Chardin .

22   Kennedy, Robert F., University of Cape Town, South Africa,
     N.U.S.A.S. "Day of Affirmation" Speech June 6th, 1966

23   Rumi, Jalal al-Din, from his poem *Those You Are With,*
     translated by John Moyne and Coleman Barks, in *Open
     Secret: Versions of Rumi,* Threshold Books, Putney VT,
     1984, p. 80

24   Washburn, *Socrates: The Well-Ordered Soul and the Moral
     Paradoxes,*
     abacus.bates.edu/~mimber/athlit02/lecture5.1.htm

25   Damiani, Anthony, *Looking into Mind,* Larson Publications, N.Y., 1990, p. 181 (Anthony was a student of Paul Brunton, astrology, Plotinus, Plato, and much more. He created the philosophic center near Ithaca called Wisdom's Goldenrod)

26   This insight is taken from Alfred North Whitehead. See especially, *Modes of Thought*, MacMillan Publishing, Canada, 1968

27   Ibid.

28   Ibid., p. 148

29   Sloan, Douglas, p. 201

30   May, Rollo, *Love and Will,* W.W. Norton, New York, 1969, p. 236

31   Quoted in Malin, Shimon, *Nature Loves to Hide*, Oxford University Press, Oxford, UK, 2001, p. 31-32. (Shimon is a theoretical physicist who taught at Colgate University for many years. This book shows the influence of western philosophy and spirituality on physics, much like Capra's 'Tao of Physics' described eastern influences)

32   see Whitehead, Alfred North, *Modes of Thought*

33   Larsen, p. 5

34   Ghose, Sri Aurobindo, *Thoughts and Aphorisms,* 1913

35   Pascal, Blaise, *Pensees,* Penguin Books, New York, 1987, p. 85

36   see Sloan, p. 72

37   Ibid, p. 8

38   Lipton, Bruce, *Biology and Belief,* Hay House; 10th Anniversary Edition (October 13, 2015) (kindle) p 85

[39] Siegel, Bernie, *Love, Medicine and Miracles*, Harper and Row, NY, 1986, p 150

[40] Simonton, Carl O. and Matthews-Simonton, Stephanie, *Getting Well Again,* Bantam Books, NY, 1984, p 150

[41] Siegel, p. 181

[42] Carter, Jimmy, *Losing My Religion for Equality,* 2009, http://www.theage.com.au/federal-politics/losing-my-religion-for-equality-20090714-dk0v.html?stb=fb

[43] See Needleman, Jacob, *The American Soul: Rediscovering the Wisdom of the Founders,* Jeremy P. Tarcher, NY, 2003, for more on this topic

[44] Washington, George, "Rules of Civility and Decent Behaviour in Company and Conversation," Rule #110, 1744

[45] Douglass, Frederick, *What to a slave is the fourth of July?* An address delivered in Rochester, NY on July 5, 1852. In *The Frederick Douglass Papers,* series 1, "Speeches, Debates, and Interviews", vol.2, 1847-54, New Haven, Yale University Press, 1982, p. 368

[46] Ibid, p. 383

[47] Ibid, p. 384

[48] Madison, James, *The Federalist* No. 10, in *The Federalist Papers: Hamilton, Madison, Jay,* with an Introduction by Clinton Rossiter, The New American Library of World Literature, 1961, p. 77

[49] Ibid., p. 78

[50] Ibid, p. 79

[51] Ibid

[52] Emerson, Ralph Waldo, "The Oversoul", in Emerson: Essays and Lectures, ed. By Joel Porte, Library of America, NY, 1983, pp. 383-400

[53] Kennedy, John Fitzgerald, in his Acceptance of the New York Liberal Party Nomination, September 14, 1960

[54] See, e.g., "Genome-wide scan demonstrates significant linkage for male sexual orientation," Sanders, Martin, Beecham, et. al., in *Psychological Medicine*, Volume 45, Issue 07, May 2015, pp 1379-1388, Cambridge University Press (available online at: http://journals.cambridge.org/action/displayAbstract;jsession id=0A999F023F3A9C4BEFAC338A4C157453.journals?aid =9625997&fileId=S0033291714002451)

[55] Hanauer, Nick, in a video available at https://www.youtube.com/watch?v=93TxokBfIlo

[56] "Four out of 5 U.S. adults struggle with joblessness, near poverty or reliance on welfare for at least parts of their lives, a sign of deteriorating economic security and an elusive American dream." 2013 The Associated Press

[57] Blankenhorn, David, *Fatherless America: Confronting Our Most Urgent Social Problem*, Harper Perennial, New York, 1996, p. 225

[58] Confucius, *Analects XV.24* (tr. David Hinton)

[59] *A Late Period Hieratic Wisdom Text: P. Brooklyn 47.218.135*, Richard Jasnow, p. 95, University of Chicago Press, 1992

[60] Diogenes Laërtius, "The Lives and Opinions of Eminent Philosophers", I, 36

[61] Brihiaspati, *Mahabharata*, Book 13, (Anusasana Parva, Section CXIII, Verse 8)

[62] (From the *Hadith*) Donaldson, Dwight M. 1963. Studies in Muslim Ethics, p.82. London S.P.C.K

63   Talmud, *Shabbat* 31a, *"The Great Principle"*

64   From *The Second Coming,* poem by William Butler Yeats, written in 1919 in the aftermath of the First World War

65   Horn, Alexander Francis, *In Search of a Solar Hero,* Element Books, UK, 1987, p xii. (Horn's brilliant Introduction to his play inspired this section and much else.)

66   Frankl, Victor, *Man's Search for Meaning,* p 86

67   I am indebted for this insight to Dr. Norman Cohen of Hebrew Union College, who spoke at *Hevreh of Southern Berkshire,* summer, 2007

68   Southern Poverty Law Center, *Intelligence Report, Spring 2012, Issue Number 145*

69   Mark Potok, February 17, 2016 https://www.splcenter.org/fighting-hate/intelligence-report/2016/year-hate-and-extremism

70   see http://www.washingtonpost.com/news/post-nation/wp/2015/05/30/hundreds-gather-in-arizona-for-armed-anti-muslim-protest/

71   *The Life and Works of Thomas Paine.* Edited by William M. Van der Weyde. Patriots' Edition. 10 vols. New Rochelle, N.Y.: Thomas Paine National Historical Association, 1925

72   Letter from George Washington to the Jewish community in Newport, RI, (1790)

73   *Works of Thomas Jefferson,* Vol. I, p 45

74   *Memorial and Remonstrance Against Religious Assessments,* James Madison, 1785 (http://religiousfreedom.lib.virginia.edu/sacred/madison_m&r_1785.html)

[75] *Memoirs of Dr. Joseph Priestly to the Year 1795,* Vol I, E Hemsted, London, 1806   A facsimile of the original is at http://books.google.com/books?id=ti46AAAAcAAJ&pg=PA 90&lpg=PA90&dq=Priestly,+%E2%80%9CIt+is+much+to+ be+lamented+that+a+man+%22&source=bl&ots=E9pTalZ5 5n&sig=MFWIcGxD6rdj7VMH99OtIP_oLgY&hl=en&sa= X&ei=A1ssUOuMCMWGyQHIyICABQ&ved=0CGYQ6A EwBQ#v=onepage&q=Priestly%2C%20%E2%80%9CIt%2 0is%20much%20to%20be%20lamented%20that%20a%20m an%20%22&f=false

[76] Paine, Thomas, *The Age of Reason,* pp. 8,9 (Republished 1984, Prometheus Books, Buffalo, NY)

[77] Schwartz, Barry, *George Washington: The Making of an American Symbol,* New York Press, 1987, pp. 174-175

[78] Franklin, Benjamin, *The Autobiography,* 1817, p 27

[79] Boller, Paul F. Jr., *George Washington & Religion,* Southern Methodist University Press: Dallas, 1963, p. 92

[80] Ibid.

[81] Thomas Jefferson: in a speech to the Virginia Baptists, 1808

[82] Kruse, Kevin M., *A Christian Nation? Since When?* Op Ed piece in the New York Times, Saturday, March 14, 2015. (Kruse, a Professor of History at Princeton, University, is the author of *One Nation Under God: How Corporate America Invented Christian America.*)

[83] Ibid.

[84] Barrows, Rev. John Henry, ed., *The World's Parliament of Religions,* Vol I, Parliament Pub. Co., Chicago, 1893, p.75

[85] Quoted in Chetanananda, Swami, *Vivekananda: East Meets West,* Vedanta Society, St. Louis, 1995

[86] Mukerji, Dhan Gopal, *The Face of Silence*, E. P. Dutton & Co., NY, 1926, p.59

[87] Ibid., p.60

[88] Augustine St., *Retract.*, I, xiii, 3

[89] Mukerji, p. 60

[90] Emerson, *Self-Reliance*

[91] Chetanananda, p. 75

[92] This and the following story are recounted in Niebuhr, Gustav, *Beyond Tolerance*, Penguin Books, NY, 2008, p.133-134

[93] All quotes from the Qur'an are from *The Message of the Qur'an*, translated by Mohammad Asad, The Book Foundation, Bristol, UK, 2003

[94] See, e.g., Khaled Abou El Fadl et.al., *The Place of Tolerance in Islam*, Beacon Press, Boston, 2002

[95] Mead, Walter Russell, *God and Gold*, Alfred A. Knopf, NY, 2007, p. 369 (A very interesting account of the history of the English speaking peoples and their influence on the world)

[96] New York Times, Right *Steps on Military Sexual Assault*, April 17, 2012, http://www.nytimes.com/2012/04/18/opinion/right-steps-on-sexual-assault-in-the-military.html

[97] King, Martin Luther, Jr., *A Christmas Sermon on Peace*, delivered at the Ebenezer Baptist Church, Dec 24, 1967

[98] Merton, Thomas, *Conjectures of a Guilty Bystander*, Image Books, 1968, p. 154

[99] Berry, Thomas, *The Great Work: Our Way into the Future*, Crown Publishing Group, Kindle Edition, 2011

[100] A. R. Orage, quoted in C. S. Nott, *Teachings of Gurdjieff: A Pupil's Journal*, Samuel Weiser, ME, 1974, p. 207

[101] Berry, Ibid.

[102] Ibid.

[103] Einstein, Albert, *Out of my Later Years*, Kensington Publishing Corp., NY, 1956, p. 9

[104] Schacker, Michael, *Global Awakening*, Park Street Press, VT, 2013 (An excellent analysis of history and coming changes)

[105] The Prophet Mohammad: Hadith

[106] Pope John Paul II, *Crossing the Threshold of Hope*, Alfred A. Knopf, NY, 1994, p. 20

[107] Hitchens, Christopher, *Political Animal*, in *Arguably: Selected Essays by Christopher Hitchens*, Signal/McClelland & Stewart, Ontario, Canada, 2011, p. 111

[108] Einstein, Albert, *Letter to Robert S. Marcus*, 1950

[109] Quoted in Holton, Gerald, and Elkana, Yehuda, *Albert Einstein, Historical and Cultural Perspectives*, Princeton University Press, Princeton, NJ, 1982, p. 300

[110] Darwin, Charles, *The Descent of Man: Selection in Relation to Sex*, 2nd ed., rev., John Murray, London, 1877, p. 130

[111] Edison, Thomas A., quoted in *The Extended Circle: A Dictionary of Humane Thought*, by Jon Wynne-Tyson, Open Gate Press, 1985, p. 75 (attributed to an 1890 Harper's Magazine article, however the quote is disputed)

[112] Quoted in *Women in History*. Rachel Carson biography. Last updated: 1/16/2013. OH, http://www.womeninhistoryohio.com/rachel-carson.html

211

113 Schopenhauer, Arthur, as quoted in *Animal Revolution: Changing Attitudes Towards Speciesism*, by Richard Ryder, Oxford, Berg Publishers, 2000, p. 57.

114 Kant, Immanuel, *Lectures on Ethics*, Cambridge University Press, 1997, p. 212, "Of Duties to animals and Spirits"

115 Schweitzer, Albert. This quote can be found dozens of times on the internet with no citation that I have been able to find.

116 Singer, Isaac Bashevis, in his Introduction to *Vegetarianism, a Way of Life*, by Dudley Giehl

117 Voltaire, in his *Philosophical Dictionary*

118 Bentham, Jeremy, *The Science of Morality*, from the MSS. of J. Bentham ed. by J. Bowring (1834 edition)

119 Camus, Albert, *The Plague,* Vintage International, NY, 1991 (first published by Alfred A. Knopf, 1948), pp. 252-253

120 Singer, Isaac Bashevis, in his short story "The Letter Writer" that appeared in *The New Yorker*, January 13, 1968.

121 James, William, "The Moral Equivalent of War," essay reprinted in *Securing the Planet,* edited by Don Carlson and Craig Comstock, Jeremy P. Tarcher, LA, 1986, p. 71

122 Ibid., p. 83

123 Schell, Jonathan, *The Fate of the Earth,* Avon Books, NY, 1982, p. 24

124 Frankl, *Man's Search for Meaning,* p. 179

125 de Chardin, Teilhard, "The Evolution of Chastity" in *Toward the Future*, Collins, London, 1975, p. 86-87

126 Kubler-Ross, Elizabeth, *On Death and Dying,* MacMillan Publishing Co., NY, 1969, p. 5

[127] Castaneda, Carlos, *Journey to Ixtlan*, Washington Square Press, NY, 1972, pp. 236-237

ABOUT THE AUTHOR

Dr. Andrew Cort is an author, speaker, teacher (mathematics and physics), attorney, doctor of chiropractic, and interfaith minister. He received his BA and MA from Colgate University, his Doctor of Chiropractic Degree from New York Chiropractic College, his Law Degree from Boston College Law School, and he was ordained by All Faiths Seminary, International.

His talks, writings and seminars encompass Spirituality, Interfaith Religion, Science, Mythology, Education, Healing, and how these all interact with each other and with contemporary culture.

He is also the Joseph Campbell Scholar and Interfaith Chaplain with *The Center for Symbolic Studies*, New Paltz, NY.

Please visit Dr. Cort's Website at
www.AndrewCort.com
and his Blog
INTERFAITH AWAKENING
www.InterfaithAwakening.com

Andrew Cort lives in Woodstock, NY, where he practices chiropractic. He is available for talks and seminars as well as officiating weddings, and can be contacted at:
Andrew@AndrewCort.com

May we have peace on Earth,
goodwill toward all men, women, and especially children,
and all that lives and breathes.

Made in the USA
Middletown, DE
22 December 2016